SOCIALISM EXPOSED

WILLIAM W. FIGLEY

Table Of Contents

PROLOGUE

Where there is no vision, the people perish.
- Proverbs 29:18

People and nations always move in the direction of their vision. Knowing that this is true, it is then absolutely crucial for us (as voters) to know exactly what vision each party or leader holds, for it will show us the direction in which they will take this country! And, as you will read, we dare not simply take words at face value. It's time we take a deeper look and decide what kind of future we want for us, and for our children and grandchildren.

If there is one concept that is pivotal for the future direction of our country in deciding for whom to vote, I believe it would be to keep the following uppermost in our minds:

The candidate can be no stronger than the platform on which he / she stands.

Sure, any candidate might sound reasonable, or claim to be on your side, but what is stated in the platform of the party they represent? This is crucial to know in order to vote wisely! Regardless of what the slick ads on TV might say, the candidate can be no stronger than the platform upon which they stand.

This book will pull back the curtain to see socialism for what it is, and where this philosophy has taken us as a nation. We will examine many facets of socialism, including the characteristics of those who espouse it, the traits of a socialist, and 9 ways to spot one. We will also show you the opposite form of governing – government by the people, which is the bedrock upon which our country was founded.

Far from a boring history manual, the explosive information laid out in this book will clarify for you how best to protect your individual freedoms, enjoy the best opportunities for your success and prosperity, and provide compelling reasons to choose life, liberty and the pursuit of happiness for you, your children, your grandchildren and your great-grandchildren.

How I've Seen Things Change Over My Lifetime

I am currently a 92-year old World War II Navy veteran, and am still very active as a professional musician and writer. I am father to 6, grandfather to 21, and great-grandfather to 38. I feel like I know a thing or two, because I've lived long enough to see a lot more than a thing or two! I've easily spotted trends during particular times of my life - trends that have led to a current culture very different from the one in which I grew up. I have been a student of politics and government for many years, and have observed subtle as well as blatant shifts in culture and policy. The changes I have seen and experienced during my lifetime would include the following:

Times were much simpler when I was a young boy. I can remember growing up, mostly in Southeastern Ohio in the days before today's modern refrigerators. We had plain, old iceboxes, about the size of a small refrigerator, and not well insulated. Each home would order ice once per week by placing a sign in their window - "ice today," and the Iceman would come in a pickup type truck and deliver a 25-pound block of ice. A very small piece of ice would usually remain from the prior trip. Food placed in these iceboxes was severely limited. We would also have milk delivered by posting a sign in our window, and we would leave the clean milk bottles on our front porch for pickup.

Having grown up in a poor area of Southeastern Ohio, there were few farms because of hard clay soil. But there were many coal miners. Miners would check downtown in a designated upper floor window for signs telling which mines (by number) were working the next day. I guess you could call this a very early version of news by "social media"!

Changes In Our Country And Changes In People

As I look back over time to observe the U.S.A. politically, I saw the signs of socialism develop in the administration of Franklin D. Roosevelt during the Depression, which extended from 1927 through much of the 1930s. In very hard times, the WPA (which stands for Works Projects Administration) provided work and help for quite a few people. What Roosevelt would have done with our government had World War II not come along, we will not know. My dad certainly did not approve of the WPA, and plenty of sarcastic jokes were passed around about the ineptitude of this government system. But times were hard, and at least it seemed like an attempt to help in some manner.

I have also seen a lot of changes in our so-called fundamentalist churches, particularly Methodist and Presbyterian churches (considered by many to be bedrock conservative in my younger days). Some of these groups and others like them began to slide away from the Old Time Gospel to give primary attention to social issues and opinions. At the same time, I observed the Federal Government increasingly involving itself in matters that should belong to the states.

World War II and its effects (both during and after the war) clouded the issue for some period of time. By the time the War ended, the church in many regards had begun to lose some of its outreach and influence.

Following World War II, there seemed to be an ever-increasing movement toward secularism. However, in my local area, the Billy Graham influence was quite strong. I participated locally in his crusades and movies as a young husband, college grad, and professional man. These crusades were "pockets of hope" in downtrodden communities and were a highlight of my young adult life.

With the rise in secularism after World War II, there was also subtle trending of the Federal Government to expand in scope and become more essential to various groups of people in the United States. I define "secularism" as a way of life that veers away from religion and faith, and trends toward self without God, and the living of one's life without serious worship or serious thought.

I do not think that the church alone is to blame for these changes. I think World War II and its aftermath had much to do with secularism.

All churches (and what they were allowed to say about their government) took a big hit when President Lyndon Johnson proposed his amendment that was passed through Congress limiting the free speech of all churches about government and political matters. To violate this unconstitutional ruling meant churches and ministries were threatened with losing their tax-exempt status. It is not difficult to see that this was a blatant attempt to shut down the voice of the church relating to political matters and how the country should be run. Lyndon Johnson was clearly a socialist masquerading as a friend of the poor and downtrodden. This country suffered greatly from his policies of big government.

Under former president Obama and his so-called "government," the churches in the U.S.A., (of whatever variety) had little relevance to the Federal Government in power. Secularism increased so much under Mr. Obama's eight years in office as to be nauseating to the extreme. Liberalism in the form of rank socialism was the order of the day during his tenure. Although saddened, I was not surprised because Mr. Obama exhibited no spiritual beliefs that I have observed to be worthy of modeling.

The truth is that socialism is opposed to Christianity as well as common sense. With a new president having just assumed power in 2017, we will see if sanity and common sense can prevail once again in our government and in our thinking.

It is my sincere and honest opinion as a 92-year old veteran, who has fought through the worst war in U.S. history, that unless we go back to the Constitution and its roots as a nation, we will surely dwindle down to Third World status.

> **Unless we go back to the Constitution and its roots as a nation, we will surely dwindle down to Third World status.**

Whenever a president and his political party hold an ideology - which to them is more important and valuable than the welfare of the people they serve - we have socialism and dictatorship. Mr. Obama's rule was a prime example of this.

If I may leave a final word of advice to all legal voters and everyone who resides in the U.S.A. - If you say hello to liberalism and welcome socialism with open arms - watch out, people!

But say hello to Constitutional principles - and welcome back personal freedoms and opportunities!

I refer you to a well-known story from our young country's history. Important leaders from each of the thirteen colonies were meeting together to determine what kind of government they would establish for our country as they were finally free from the strangling and oppressive rule of England.

A lady walked up to Benjamin Franklin after the convention and said - ***"Ben, what kind of government have you given us?"***

And Franklin replied: ***"A Republic - if you can keep it!"***

What a statement that was!!

The plain fact of the matter is this – we can see that our country has drifted away from our founding ideals by drifting away from the great principles of the Constitution, which guarantees our basic freedoms.

With a truly conservative administration having recently assumed power, I do not see our country dwindling into Third World status. Not under President Trump. *But socialism, if and when it is allowed to gain more ground in our country, will kill our nation and with it, will strangle the hopes and dreams of all decent Americans.*

A Personal Word to the Reader

This book was written out of the passion of my convictions – beliefs that were honed and sharpened during my days as a serviceman in the U.S. Navy during World War II. I fought for freedom then – risking my life daily along with thousands of other U.S. soldiers in the heat of battle. Sadly, my best friend and many other fellow soldiers never made it back home. They paid the ultimate sacrifice for our freedom. I hold them in high esteem, and have vowed to spend the rest of my life fighting for the freedoms they died to protect.

My goal in writing this book is to paint a crystal clear picture of what socialism is, its characteristics, the traits of a socialist and how you can become adept at discerning those operating with this philosophy (whether overtly or covertly). I have seen more and more of the slippery slope of socialism take root in this country over the past several decades, and I am sounding a warning. Just as I was selected to blow my trumpet for "Reveille" bright and early every morning to wake up the troops (and they weren't always happy about it), I am sounding a warning call now to wake up the Patriots before it is too late! If war teaches you anything about an enemy, it is that this enemy can sneak up on you and wipe out your entire battalion (before you even know what happened) if you are not always vigilant and at the ready. The enemy who sneaks into the camp pretending to be on your side is the worst of traitors and puts the lives of many good people in peril.

Socialism is no less dangerous than the enemy I have just described. It is absolutely vital that we learn to recognize how to spot the characteristics – discern the enemy tactics – and prevent this deadly, suffocating siren call of the Left from slithering any further into our camp and stealing every freedom we still have remaining. Whether we like it or not, we are in a battle to save our great Republic – we are in a war to retain the freedoms that your parents, grandparents and great grandparents risked their lives to protect. Many paid the ultimate price to give us our freedom. May history look back on this period of time and proclaim - without reservation - that we, as modern day Patriots, gave our best and made them proud.

A Timely Word About the Generations

I was born during the time of those who are now called "The Greatest Generation." I am honored to be a part of this generation. Perhaps it is easy for some to see how my convictions have developed as a result of my background, my time in the service and my age. Yet my goal is not to reach just the older generation with this critical message, but ALL generations. And believe me, my generation is not the only one who sees the slippery slide into socialism and the havoc it will wreak for those who allow this philosophy to prevail.

Allow me to introduce my great nephew, Patrick Croke, a contributing author to this book. His thought-provoking chapter is found in the Intermission section. Patrick will specifically address the Millennial generation (and younger) as a Millennial himself. He will clearly and compellingly illustrate why socialism contradicts the very values that the younger generation embrace. I encourage you to read his words carefully and thoughtfully. This young man is a brilliant thinker and speaker and I have no doubt that he will hold political office one day.

Amazingly, Patrick and I have never had the privilege of meeting. We live in different states, are quite busy with our respective commitments, and only recently became aware of the passion with which each of us approaches this current political era. We both see the *promises* (of turning back to the values of our Constitution) and the *pitfalls* of a stronghold of socialism in our country. Through a series of amazing, unexpected events, we became aware of our singular passion to educate our fellow citizens (young to old) of the dangers of socialism. I believe it was a divine connection.

Our goal is to highlight the roots of our Republic and inspire modern-day Patriots to fight to preserve the freedoms so many brave Americans have given their lives to protect.

From the very young, to the Millennial Generation, and spanning the decades to the Greatest Generation, may we take a stand and fight for our freedoms, turn our nation right side up again, and may God bless America!

We hold these truths to be self-evident; that all men are created equal and endowed by their Creator with certain unalienable Rights, and among these are Life, Liberty, and the Pursuit of Happiness.
~ The Declaration of Independence

INTRODUCTION

A Brief Glimpse Into the History
of the United States of America

The God who gave us life,
gave us liberty at the same time.
~ Thomas Jefferson

Your Government and Your Freedom

There is now, and always has been, a direct relationship between your government and your freedom, beginning with the particular type of government you reside under and the freedoms you are guaranteed under that type of government.

It's important that we understand the foundational concepts of the 3 major types of government in precise terms.

There are three basic types of government in world society: a republic, a dictatorship, and socialism. It is critical for us not only to clearly identify each, but to also understand the underlying principles of each type of government.

It is important to note that a "democracy" or a "republic" ***does not refer to political parties***, but to the system of government within a particular country.

We have a **Republic** in the U.S.A., which is basically a democracy within a republic. Other acceptable titles for the U.S. type of government are a Constitutional Republic or a Representative Democracy. A pure democracy cannot be achieved with a large group of people, even by states, because each person cannot vote as an individual on every issue. In a country of 300 million people, it's just not feasible to have everyone vote on everything!

You could call the U.S.A. a representative democracy if you like, and you would be equally correct. In the USA we have a legislative body - the House of Representatives and the Senate. These are elected citizens representing the huge number of people all over the country, so that each state has representation in Washington, D.C. In the executive branch we have the President, who is our leader and the Commander-in-Chief of our armed forces. And then we have the judicial branch - the court system that represents the legal arm of our government from the lowest courts to the higher courts, all the way to the highest court in the land, known as the Supreme Court.

Be on the alert here for another "wolf in sheep's clothing" regarding the socialists' use of the word "democracy." It is critical to note that the word "democracy" is not found in any of our founding documents. However, the Pledge of Allegiance and article IV of the Constitution do mention the term "Republic."

The U.S. has not been - and cannot ever be - a pure democracy, because the majority rule cannot override the individual rights of each citizen, according to the Constitution.

When you hear the Left parrot that this or that is "a threat to our democracy," you must ask yourself if they are referring to our Constitutional Republic (where the majority cannot override the rights of the individual), or are they referring to a pure democracy? They are hoping you don't know the difference! Our Founding Fathers set up our government so that we operate with some democratic principles, but within the structure of a republic. It is critical that an individual's rights cannot be violated simply by a majority vote! This is why we must abide by our Constitution. It is true that we operate with some democratic principles (where chosen representatives decide upon laws with

> **The word "democracy" is not found in any of our founding documents.**

a majority vote), but within the confines of a republic. The Republic ensures that the rule of law protects your individual rights from tyrants who desire to rule over you.

Make no mistake about it - left-leaning socialists will use the term "democracy" to try to sneak in their own agenda that violates the rights of individuals via the Constitution. We must be awake and aware!

The courts are obligated to interpret the laws and actions of people in the United States in accordance with our Constitution - our basic document pertaining to how this country was founded and the basic fundamental rights for its citizens. Once again, the United States of America was founded as a representative democracy within a republic, so the Constitution reflects this structure.

Unfortunately, our country has slipped into a degraded kind of government over the past number of years. We will address this in more depth throughout this book.

The second form of government goes by several different names - but it is the same government no matter which way you slice it. In the past, it was incorrectly labeled as communism, but is specifically known as **dictatorship** or Soviet Communism. This is the type of government system you will also find in China, North Korea, Iran, and in other places around the globe.

Calling this type of government by different names does not make it any different from what it is. With a dictatorship, usually a big group seizes the power of government - oftentimes with the direct help of the country's military - and a leader is designated. The rule of the dictator is absolute. You must surrender all your rights to the central government. If you resist, you are shot, or you disappear forever. Of course, all of the ruling class must prove that they are 100% loyal to the dictator, or they, too, are killed. What a pleasant arrangement (said with tongue in cheek)!!

We can easily see that violence may be employed to the utmost degree to establish and maintain a dictatorship. An honest look into the history of dictatorial leaders such as Hitler, Stalin, or many others, will paint a clear portrait of control by violence.

The third type of government is called **socialism**. It is actually the same as a dictatorship, but it is *never* called that, and this type of central government is established through relatively peaceful means. But don't allow the "relatively peaceful means" of control lull you into thinking this type of government is without danger. Therein lies one of our greatest threats to freedom. Let me explain.

PART I:
SOCIALISM EXPOSED!

The Door on the Left

Socialism in Democracy's Clothing

(An Accurate Picture of a Wolf in Sheep's Clothing)

Socialism is the same as communism,
only better English.
~ George Bernard Shaw

A government of socialism is typically established by *pretense* of being a "democracy."

In this scenario, the public unwittingly becomes the victim of a **con-job** -falling for the notion that they can become part of a great movement. They are assured that they will be well cared for by a *compassionate* government.

> **A government of socialism is typically established by pretense of being a "democracy."**

The leaders of this so-called movement play skillfully on the emotions of the people, and prey upon their unrealistic dreams.

But it isn't long before we observe bigger and bigger central government, an increasingly burdensome national debt (which in reality burdens everyone), fewer good jobs (usually fewer jobs of any kind), higher taxes, more government rules and regulations, and far fewer freedoms than anyone thought possible.

The ruling class under socialism is governed (if at all) by a set of rules that are designed to promote the Elite's ideas, their grand philosophy and their power,

> **Socialism means slavery.**
> **~ Lord Acton**

in addition to showing off their wealth and prestige. They need high-powered binoculars to be able to see the middle class and the poor class, and what has become of both of them. But their expertise in promoting the socialistic agenda would skin a snake in an instant.

And make no mistake, folks - just as in a dictatorship, we common folk are all in the same boat with a socialist government - we can't really expect everything we dream about for our families – utopia (they tell us) is *just* out of reach, and will always remain that way.

Take a close look at the policies of Barack Obama and the Democrat Party - we can see that our Constitution was only paid lip service by these socialist leaders. They interpreted the provisions of the Constitution in the most liberal way possible, destroying its basic provisions, as if it were a document that can be modified or changed at the will of whoever is in the driver's seat at the moment. Can you see the process at work here?

Meanwhile, government grows bigger and bigger, becoming a monster with an insatiable appetite to expand and control more and more of citizen life. The appointment of greater numbers of bureaucrats (who are unelected) are then charged with downgrading the poor and the middle class so that the Elitist leaders of this movement can grow rich!

And there is much more. Under the socialistic process, the Federal Government becomes involved in many areas that the Constitution has reserved for the states and for the people (NOT to the Federal Government)! And guess what? These areas of involvement are those that the Federal Government has no expertise - so the government in large part (for the past several decades) has been involved in areas it isn't qualified to oversee, and the voice of the people has been nearly silenced!

Lies, promises, and half-truths - these are the means by which the socialists remain in power. They dare not speak the truth that government has tried these things before and utterly failed, but it is true, nonetheless.

We will always have failure and disappointment for the public when the Federal Government becomes involved in anything that the Constitution has not specified.

The eight years of Barack Obama should have made that clear!

Back to the Basics and Back to the Founding Fathers

Now, after a rather scathing review of the policies of socialism, let us once again bring to the public eye, what our Founding Fathers knew deeply and what they said about the founding of the new nation. It is necessary to quote them from the Declaration of Independence - a document drafted as we separated from England and became the independent United States of America.

The very REASON we separated from England is now the battle cry of the socialistic agenda!

It may shock you to discover that the very REASON we separated from England is now the battle cry of the socialistic agenda!

In the Congress, July 4, 1776, the U.S. Colonies set forth this unanimous Declaration of the 13 States of America:

When in the course of human events, it becomes necessary for one people to dissolve the political bands which have connected them with another and to assume among the powers of the earth, the separate and equal station to which the Laws of Nature and of Nature's God entitle them, a decent respect to the opinions of mankind requires that they should declare the causes which impel them to the separation.

*We hold these truths to be self-evident, that all men are created equal, that they are endowed by their **Creator** with certain unalienable Rights, that among these are Life, Liberty, and the pursuit of Happiness - that to secure these rights, Governments are instituted among Men, deriving their just powers from the consent of the governed.*

"Self evident" - that is, needing no further truth or explanation. "All men are created equal "- that is, in the sight of God and in the sight of whatever physical laws that exist. "Unalienable" means that it cannot be changed or questioned.

I have some honest questions for all who read this Declaration - does a socialistic form of government fit the criteria outlined by the Declaration of Independence? Did the Founding Fathers state that we were to seek to ever increase the size of a bloated, debt-

> **The goal of socialism is communism.**
>
> **~ Vladimir Lenin, Founder of Russian Communist Party**

ridden government, controlled by the Elites, with heavier and heavier tax burdens for the common peo ple? Did our Founders intend for us to bow under the oppressive weight of government regulations - sending jobs overseas, and depriving many of us from the ability to find even an adequate means of income - forcing some to then require some level of dependence upon this same bloated government?

Does anyone truly think that a socialistic form of government fits with the ideals of our brave Founding Fathers?

The U.S.A. was Founded Upon the Idea of Individual Freedom

To be free of England and free of the overreach of cruel, kingly authority does not square, in my mind, with a government strangely similar to the one our Founding Fathers escaped from in order to create a better life for themselves and their families!

Why form a new government that is clearly the same as the one from which you escaped?

You can see that socialism is **not** what our Founding Fathers had in mind at all.

But let's go even further. I personally believe that our basic rights come from GOD – and our Founding Fathers believed this - enough that they were willing to die for it!!

If you, or any other individual, do not believe that our basic human rights come from God, then from whom or from where do they come?

Why form a new government that is clearly the same as the one from which you escaped?

The answer betrays the crooked beliefs of the socialists and the big-government fanatics. If our basic human rights on this earth do not come from God, then they must come from men.

And we know that what is _given_ by men, can also be _taken away_ by men, in the blink of an eye!

The God who gave us life,
gave us liberty at the same time.
~ Thomas Jefferson

You cannot legislate the poor into freedom by legislating the wealthy out of freedom. What one person receives without working for, another person must work for without receiving. The government cannot give to anybody anything that the government does not first take from somebody else. When half of the people get the idea that they do not have to work because the other half is going to take care of them, and when the other half gets the idea that it does no good to work because somebody else is going to get what they work for, that, my dear friend, is about the end of any nation.

You cannot multiply wealth by dividing it.

~ Dr. Adrian Pierce Rogers (1931-2005)

Let me tell you what kind of men and women the socialists want to have in power: those who believe that influence, money and power should rule everyone, and only the Elite should create the rules and force all others to abide by them! What a disaster this would be!

But Wait!! What a disaster *it has already been* for the United States for the most recent eight years of a socialistic style of presidency! It has been a stark and sad reality for those of us as citizens who live in this country and care about the integrity of our Republic.

The Hallmarks of Socialism

There are two main hallmarks of socialism. If we keep these two hallmarks uppermost in our thinking, they will greatly assist us in discerning who is operating in the socialist agenda (whether they admit it or not).

Hallmark Number I - Socialism denies our basic freedoms. Socialists do not believe that these basic rights come from God. Their form of government denies God and our God-given freedoms. If our freedoms come from God, then who can rightfully take them away? But if they come from man, then errant rulers can whisk away those "man-made" freedoms at will, with no regard for the consequences to us.

> **Socialism requires that the government becomes your god.**
> **~ Rafael Cruz**

Hallmark Number II - Socialistic governments are always big, bloated and ever expanding; and, without exception, trash and downgrade the middle class (who end up paying for the bureaucratic bloated government and lining the pockets of the Elites).

> **Giving money and power to government is like giving whiskey and car keys to teenage boys.**
> **~ P. J. O'Rourke**

Secrets of Socialism

A lie told often enough becomes the truth.
~ Vladimir Lenin, founder of the
Russian Communist Party

There is still more you need to know (and this secret will **never** be revealed by those who are promoting socialism, so you need to be aware).

What follows is one of the keys to understanding the socialistic point of view. Simply put, there is a deeply held belief that the common people don't know very much, and don't really know what is good for them. However, "they" (the socialists) know what is best for society!

Bottom line: socialists think we're idiots!

I believe a lot of people would have voted for change in our government long ago, had they really understood this truth!

Please read the next sentence very carefully, for it describes an overlooked truth of epic proportions. Socialism is deceptive and it is portrayed in such a way that it *sounds good.* So there are many who jump on the socialistic bandwagon who have <u>no idea</u> what is behind the philosophy, or how far down the road of "no return" it would take us if we allow it to overtake our government and ultimately, our country and our freedoms.

Ideology – How Does it Affect Me?

One's deeply held beliefs are called one's *ideology*. Let's discuss, for a moment, the ideology of the socialists. They idolize big government, government programs and decisions that are contrary to common sense (some would call it "horse sense"). They attempt to marginalize (or vilify) any group or movement that does not agree with them.

If you need further proof of marginalization or vilification, simply search the Internet for #Walkaway and listen to the personal (often harrowing) stories of those who dared to think for themselves and no longer parrot the Democrat/Socialist party line.

Furthermore, socialists favor and promote programs that do not work, that CANNOT work, for freedom - but as long as they are run by the Central Government, these disastrous programs are fine and dandy with the ruling Elitists!!

In plain English, socialists promote policies that not only do not work, but also infringe upon individual freedom and do not build up the poor class or the middle class.

Their ideology is placed *above* freedom, *above* common sense, and is placed *above* everything that would benefit the working class of America.

I used to believe (many years ago) that socialists just wanted to divide the wealth of the country amongst everyone. While this may be true on some level, it is by no means the only purpose of socialism. Let's continue our exposure of the ideology of socialism.

Socialistic Ideology Exposed

Socialistic ideology could be a fascinating study of an "ideal" society if it were not utterly destructive to our people and our country, particularly to our middle class, and our poor. Those who espouse socialism (or dictatorship by consent, which is exactly what it is) operate like this: their first target is the middle class - the most important class of all our citizens in this regard, because the majority of the wealth comes from the middle class (a little wealth from each of the middle class millions).

The first target of socialism is the middle class.

The socialists, through con-artistry, steal the wealth from the middle class through excessive taxation, over-reaching control, and with lofty promises, most of which will never see the light of day. Their system of control over the middle class produces a sorrowful *sameness*, limits the ceiling of accomplishment for all, siphons off any money or independence rightly belonging to the individual, and makes it well nigh impossible for nearly all middle class people to get ahead financially or in prestige.

So for the poor middle class, the hopes, dreams and aspirations of accomplishment are whisked away, and much of the middle class now becomes part of the poorer class.

What really happens to the middle class wealth that the socialists steal?

Well, some goes to benefit the very poor, making them dependent on the government for life while harvesting their votes for future election cycles. Oh, the middle class may get an occasional bone or benefit of some type, but not much. And there is no doubt that much of the money siphoned by socialism benefits the Elite - those in the shadows who control government - money they greedily grasp for themselves and their cronies. These are people you really do not know - and people you will never know. Yet your tax dollars fill their coffers.

> **Whoever controls the Middle Class of America, or any nation, absolutely controls that nation.**

The bottom line is this: Whoever controls the Middle Class of America, or any nation, absolutely controls that nation.

So you see, friend, how many greedy paws the Elite socialists already have, and how they are controlling our nation? This could be subject to change for a time, by the election of a President who values the Constitution, the Rule of Law, and the hopes and dreams of the vast middle class. It seems the sleeping giant in America is awakening and realizing that we are in danger of losing even more!

Sadly, we have been deceived as a nation by anti-American ideas and anti-American policies, as well as decades of policies that ignore both freedom and responsibility. Again, I say with sadness: anti-American ideas and policies promoted by the socialists have taken our country to the brink of destruction!

Does this mean that socialists are anti-American? You be the judge!

A Look at Another Kind of Ideology

Do conservatives and those who adhere to our country's Constitution have an ideology? Oh, yes! This ideology lines up with the Constitution and the policy rules set in place at our nation's founding, and are the very reason our nation became great in the first place! So to embrace an ideology of government and individual freedom that agrees with our Constitution and our Bill of Rights (the founding documents of the U.S.A.) is the right way to go - indeed, the only way to go!

To prove my point, let us take a look at the Preamble of the Constitution of the United States of America. Why was our country formed to begin with?

We the people of the United States, in order to form a more perfect Union, establish Justice, insure domestic Tranquility, provide for the common defense, promote the general Welfare and secure the Blessings of Liberty to ourselves and our Posterity, do ordain and establish this Constitution for the United States of America.

How's your freedom coming along, citizen? Remember - ***the type of government you have determines the amount of freedom you will enjoy.***

Only under conservatism and government by the Constitution (which the current Republican party stands for) can you have the very maximum amount of freedom for each individual in a system that also provides your neighbor and everyone else with the same amount of liberty.

Who Pays for the Experiment of Socialism?

Who pays for all the socialistic folly that has been perpetuated by the Obama administration and all of their adherents?

You do!!

Hardworking men and women desperately need a government who will listen to them, who will address their needs, their wants, their hopes and their dreams.

> **The problem with socialism is that you eventually run out of other people's money.**
> **~ Margaret Thatcher**

I have seen so many changes and "social experiments" in my 92+ years of living, and I want to say that I am extremely grateful to the Lord for giving us a new leader; a president who will make our country proud again, prosperous again and great again. A president who is prepared to listen to the American people, to lead the world with strength, and lead it in a way that does not entangle the U.S. forever in the problems of other countries.

A strong and prosperous America can then reach out to others in a way that does not cheat our own citizens of jobs, opportunities, and dreams of a better future. Is this a pretty tall order? Yes! But with the right leadership under God, it can and will be done (see Part II for more specifics).

Socialism and Freedom Do Not Mix

It is time for all who love our country to recognize that the socialistic view of government is not only a difference of opinion from those on the side of freedom under the law, but it is a _mindset_ which violates the very rule of law our country was founded upon. Pushing such a philosophy in ideology and action is treason waiting to happen. **You simply cannot have freedom and support the enemies of freedom at the same time.**

Thus, a <u>radical viewpoint</u> questioning our very form of government cannot qualify as simply a "different opinion" that must be considered as an alternative to our Constitution.

The socialistic view of law and government cannot pass the Freedom Clause found in our Declaration of Independence:

> *We hold these truths to be self-evident, that all men are created equal, that they are endowed by their Creator with certain unalienable Rights, that among theses are <u>Life, Liberty, and the Pursuit of Happiness.</u>*

Which of these rights do socialists support? The answer is **none**.

They practice big government, an Elite ruling class, a depressed middle class, joblessness, dependence, and turning your country into a system that fights against you. They operate on lies, empty promises, and yes, even hatred! The "tolerance" of the Left quickly disappears once an individual or party dares to disagree with their viewpoint on how the country ought to be run.

Where's Waldo?

(Or How to Spot a Socialist a Mile Away)

To find Waldo, you first must identify what Waldo looks like.

Although it may be difficult to separate what a person does from what they think, I will attempt to do just that.

I believe there are **9 ways to spot a socialist** or liberal from all other beliefs.

Socialism is a philosophy of failure, the creed of ignorance, and the gospel of envy; its inherent virtue is the equal sharing of misery.
~ Winston Churchill

Actions Speak Louder Than Words

Those with the socialist agenda often have smooth sounding words, but their actions betray those words. They simply hope that their words provide a smokescreen so you won't notice what they are doing. If you look closely at their actions, you will begin to see a pattern.

1. Socialists are always blaming someone or something for all the problems we have. (They claim they inherited these problems from former presidents or former leaders, etc. It makes no difference to them how long they may have had to fix the problems.) In short, they take no responsibility for any problem.

2. Socialists rarely answer a direct question about their policies, programs, or actions. "The question is always too complicated to give a direct answer," they are likely to say.

3. There is an overwhelming lack of transparency regarding the policies, programs and actions of a socialistic government. This is on purpose: socialists do **not** want people to know what is going on.

4. Socialists are guilty of deflection. How do they use deflection? They simply cite *who they are* and *what position they hold* when questioned about wrongdoing or mistakes they have made. After all, we shouldn't question their authority! They hope this absolves them of any guilt. In other words, don't expect an honest answer to a direct question!

5. Socialists typically refuse to accept blame for a failed policy or a wrong decision on their part.

6. The socialists will say that the attack, the event or incident (or whatever it is that results in loss of life or property, but especially the loss of U.S. lives) will result in "the greater good for all." This is one of the most horrific and insulting statements I have ever heard! But many such events are part of the history of socialism. Look at our brave men killed at Benghazi, for example, due to a blatant lack of protection.

7. Liberals and socialists are always true to their doctrine and/or ideology (which is deeply held beliefs) no matter what. It makes no difference what the law or common sense says; the socialist will try to make excuses for not following the law or not following common sense or long-standing precedents. The basic right to freedom (or any advantage to the U.S. citizen) is in last place with the socialist.

8. Liberals and socialists don't live under the same rules as the common people. We had in power (with former President Obama) a group of Elitists who did not live under the same laws the common people had to obey. They never intended to live under the same laws as the people they pretended to serve. And we have had eight years of socialism under Barack Obama to prove our case.

9. Smear campaigns, false accusations, delay and obstruction are all a part of the socialistic agenda. Sadly, it appears they will stop at nothing to get their own way and will rule with an iron fist if that is what it takes to ramrod their policies down the throats of the American people. If you doubt that for a moment, just recall Justice Brett Kavanaugh's recent confirmation hearings. One of our most sacred procedures involving a nomination to the Supreme Court of the United States was commandeered by the Leftists to look more like a circus act than a solemn assembly.

The truth is, there is a ***recognizable pattern of thinking and acting*** that is always going to be a part of the socialist's makeup. It is not good to ignore the signs, folks.

The ideology of a person is the sum total of his/her deeply held beliefs. You might call them personal or private beliefs. But don't be surprised to see how quickly these "private" beliefs jump right into government policy, which will then affect *your* personal behavior and freedoms. Once put into office, the socialist's personal beliefs won't be private for very long.

The 9 Traits of a Socialist

Egotism, one-sided thinking, an Ivory Tower mentality and selfishness are an integral part of the socialistic belief system. These people possess a feel-good mentality and are do-gooders only to the extent that it serves their purposes. Socialists thrive on fantasy in their ideology, often act childishly, and are chillingly deficient in good old common sense.

You will soon be able to see how the basic characteristics or traits of the socialist can impact government, personal thinking, and actions, and how very destructive these actions can be. But typically thought comes before actions. The thought process of a socialist is incomplete, one-sided, and never lives up to reality. A globalist viewpoint of government is their norm.

Let's now expound upon each of the 9 traits and describe the effects of this type of governing on your Constitutional freedoms.

Egotism

The governmental socialist thinks he is the greatest and his opinions and solutions are far better than those of the "right-wing fanatics." "Those out-of-date Constitutionalists - away with them!!"

Does the socialist think he or she knows best how to run a government? Of course! Now I submit to you that egotism also has much to do with a bloated government and its effects on business, jobs, and so forth. What did the previous eight years of the Obama administration teach us as American citizens? Who seizes more control when factories leave, jobs become more and more scarce, and many are forced to depend on welfare to simply survive?

An egotist never wants to admit a wrong even though the terrible effects of this wrong are in our faces! An egotist is almost always a one-sided person: It is "his way or the highway!"

Chuck Schumer, a senator from New York (and others like him) have the gall to say that conservatives are not mainstream in U.S. thinking, when the truth is that socialists view anything or anyone outside the socialistic point of view as being out of the mainstream.

One-Sided Thinking

This is a very dangerous system of thinking, especially for governing a wonderful country. It promotes big government and trashes law and order. The socialist believes (whether they admit it or not) in a governmental system opposed to law and order.

A one-sided thinking system leads us to the failure of the socialists to keep the very first duty of our Federal

Government - which is to provide for the common defense.

A one-sided thinking system puts the socialists in the wrong concerning immigration and the foremost duty of our government - to secure peace and safety for our citizens.

We cannot secure our citizens in peace and safety if we let into our country, people who cannot properly be vetted. The socialist says, "We don't want borders or walls - this is not who we are."

But, dear people, it is not "who we are" to throw citizens safety open to thugs, killers and criminals. "Who we are" are citizens who abide by the laws of our land - first of all to provide for the common defense. It makes no difference whether the threat is an army, or a killer on the loose!

If you don't have life, you won't need liberty, and you can't pursue happiness!

The second and third duties of the Federal Government are to promote the general welfare and to secure the blessings of liberty both to us and to our posterity.

Many citizens have been harmed or killed by illegal immigrants. Although many of these criminal aliens have been deported numerous times, they have subsequently entered illegally, once again.

Simply put, if you don't have life, you won't need liberty, and you can't pursue happiness!

Ivory Tower Mentality

Ah, the socialists are in their Ivory Tower, the elevated place where they rule as kings and queens, and nothing else matters. "We are so high above you with our socialistic power and globalist governing – and now that we are in power, your petty problems and complaints can be dismissed out of hand. After all, since we are your kings and rulers, we obviously know what is best for you!"

Selfishness

This is self-explanatory. A selfish person wants their own way about everything, regardless of the effects that "their own way" may have on society. This fits hand in glove with egotism.

A selfish person should not be running our government. After all, the obvious definition of a "public servant" should be a person who thinks about and cares for the people whom he or she represents. A selfish person won't obey law and order, either.

Feel Good Mentality

Do not think for a moment that the socialist doesn't have this type of mentality. He is full of it! A feel-good mentality involves some fantasy as well. This type of thinking never squares up with truth, safety or common sense. If something feels good, let's do it!

"We will be the King of the Road, riding high on our own version of 'wonderful accomplishments.' As we expand government power and take more of your rights and money away, we will proclaim these accomplishments in glowing terms, and those opposed to us will be ashamed."

It undoubtedly would feel good to some people (and to all socialists) to have no walls or borders to our country. "Why, we would be the model country to envy for ages to come," the socialists say.

We must open our eyes! The immigrants we let into America will vote to keep these socialists in office forever! Folks, this shouldn't sound crazy, because it is part of the feel-good mentality. Feel-Gooders will destroy a country. They will never improve it.

If we insist on following a feel-good mentality, we will end up being a third world country, with no laws for anyone but the selfish haters. I think back to the sixties and the folk songs of *Peter, Paul & Mary*, and I can hear: "Where have all the *freedoms* gone?"

You will remember that most of their folk-type songs were asking where the old values and the old, commonsense honest folks had gone.

My friends, it is time for us to hold on to our <u>real</u> heroes - real law-abiding examples of honest man and womanhood. They will disappear one by one in a third-world socialistic country: the rights, the laws, the godly examples - and one day we could be singing: "Where have all the kind folks gone? And where have all the values gone? And *Where have all the honest folks gone?"*

Do-Gooders

These do-gooders are the same ones with the feel-good mentality – yet we must be aware that socialists will be do-gooders only to the extent that they help themselves and their image with the public, and very little beyond that. And be aware - how they come across and what they promise during an election cycle can change in a hot flash once they assume power.

Fantasy

We all know what fantasy is - it's thinking that everything will somehow become magically wonderful and fantastically good for everyone. This goes along with one-sided thinking. Only a system of law and order with respect for the rights of others can endure. This isn't fantasy – it is reality! If you want a country where people are blessed, yes, blessed beyond belief, yet also have freedom within limits, we must allow others their freedom within the law. Fantasy is **not** (and will never be) reality.

Childishness

Boy, have we ever seen this trait displayed in the aftermath of the presidential election of 2016! I have never in my lifetime heard or seen such childish reactions to the loss of an election. And I have lived a long time. Now I understand that one will be either disappointed or ecstatic over an election, especially a presidential election. What is neither understood, nor welcomed, is whining, crying and lamenting over the fact that their presidential candidate lost the election. Never mind how or who! "We expected to have dear Hillary as our next president! Oh, this just cannot be! The election must have been rigged, or something went wrong on Mars," or some other ridiculous statement.

And, oh yes, there were demonstrations, riots, destruction of property, broken laws, and violence against people who participated in the election of Trump – the despised candidate that the Left has still not gotten over.

Oh but wait! We see at some colleges and universities, those who will step in and be kind and generous. Look at our poor students - distraught, terrified, and stunned with disbelief - let's bring out the hot cocoa, the coloring books and the crayons. Let's set these poor students down and comfort them - cancel classes for a week - mourn with the students! Oh, let's become part of their tragedy!

Politician, student, or professor – it's the same mentality, played out differently, but amounting to the same thing – "We hate what has happened. Our country is lost, our hope is gone - we can never…" and on and on. Did the Republicans act this way in 2008 and in 2012 when Obama won these elections? Of course not!

Now dear reader, take a close look at the characteristics and at the traits of the socialist - if you are honest, what do you find? You find traits and characteristics that cannot and will not govern with fairness and with respect. You will hopefully understand that such traits can never restore a nation to greatness again, nor establish principles that will do what is right and fair for all citizens.

Dear people, socialists, who could never have founded a nation like ours, certainly cannot restore to our nation the greatness it once had. Note that I did not say perfection, but greatness.

Am I saying that a socialist should never hold high office nor govern? That is exactly what I am saying. I hate their policies - not them as individuals. Our own laws, common sense, and the Word of God all allow hatred of the results of destructive beliefs, but not hatred of the people who hold them.

Allow President Trump and elected Conservatives some space. We allowed Obama space for eight years! Vote in the midterm elections for true Patriots, who will uphold our Constitution and our precious freedoms.

Lack of Common Sense

Believe it or not, lack of common sense is a trait that is endlessly perpetuated in socialistic belief and action. There are many policies and regulations now on the books that do not make a lot of sense. As business owners

> **Socialists, who could never have founded a nation like ours, certainly cannot restore to our nation the greatness it once had.**

can attest, the hassle of foolish regulations has caused many an honest business to close its doors.

Some of our governmental procedures need to be revisited and modified, because they cause delay in creating positive momentum. I am referring specifically to the Senate and House of Representatives and the laws they have an opportunity to pass. It certainly appears that some of these procedures for governing and passing laws are too time-consuming and cumbersome and end up causing needless confusion and delay.

Common sense is something that socialists (and most leftist liberals) have in short supply. I define common sense as good and honorable conclusions that shouldn't need an act of Congress to get accomplished.

Many a parent has said: "He doesn't have enough sense to come in out of the rain!" If it is raining outside and you are sure to get soaked, it would be common sense to wear a raincoat, carry an umbrella, and perhaps even go inside to avoid getting wet. And in some cases, doing the above is wise to prevent catching a cold. It would not be common sense to stand out in the rain and get soaked with water and then to endure the consequences of your decision.

Now what does this have to do with the socialist? Simply this - a socialist does not operate with common sense as most conservatives do, because the ideology of socialism is contrary to common sense. Socialistic ideology is contrary to conservative principles, and ultimately contrary to our basic Constitutional rights and to our guaranteed protection from harm and danger (which are guaranteed under the Constitution).

In very brief terms, the ideology of a socialist ignores common sense. Socialism promotes a governmental system that elevates white-collar crime, protects only the ruling Elite, and trashes the rights of legal citizens in regard to safety, protection and the right to pursue happiness.

If there is not some common sense in governing,
there can be no law and order,
no basic human rights, no safety,
and you can forget about pursuing happiness.

INTERMISSION

A Word to the Millennial Generation (and younger) from a Millennial

By Patrick Croke

A Youthful Perspective

I am honored to have the opportunity to inject my ideas into this book. I would like to thank my great-uncle, William Figley, for not only providing me a platform to speak my mind, but also for his service many years ago in a time of human history that not even myself, nor my peers, can truly appreciate.

Opportunity

In today's volatile political climate, it is quite difficult to decide which beliefs are worth entertaining, and which ones are not. Of course, there are beliefs that are passed down from your parents; but beliefs are never static, and a principle of effective growth is evidenced through the questioning of the belief systems that have enveloped you since the dawn of your worldly understanding. As we grow up and begin to question our society and ourselves more and more, we are simultaneously developing our own dynamic belief systems correlating to the lens of perception by which we view the world. That lens is a critical component in how we will interpret the information to which you and I are exposed.

In my youth, I lacked the fortunate circumstances of many of my peers. I quickly realized that if I were to ever achieve the things I wanted, I was going to have to work hard and smart for them. When I got to high school, many of my friends were simply given vehicles. This was not the case for me. I went out and got a job at the local grocery store and bagged items until I finally had enough saved up to buy my own vehicle. I achieved such a goal because I told myself I could, and I went out and did it. Not only was able to purchase my own car, but I had a good amount of money in my bank account (and I haven't looked back, either). I went from the kid labeled as "poor" and "moocher" to treating my friends to occasional meals and supporting myself without my parents' help. These events culminated into my perceptive lens of how I saw America, allowing me to appreciate the fact that I could just about do *whatever the hell I wanted* if I worked for it.

My story may mean very little, but what *does* carry weight was the realization that I could achieve the goals I set out for myself, even in the face of such difficult circumstances. Such a mindset involved the understanding that I need NOT blame my life circumstances for my problems, because I, as a person, can change them. This is exactly the kind of mindset that our country was founded and based upon. My story is just a minute example of the kind of medium that America provides: one with equal *opportunity.* This is the beauty of the country we live in: our governmental framework establishes institutions to allow individual freedom, and thus opportunity. Such a framework is the antithesis of the socialist economic principles that a surprising number of youth seem to identify with today.

An essential point to establish is that equal opportunity does NOT imply equal outcome. It seems as though many young people have misconstrued what it means to live and grow up in this nation (much less this world). Many expect external factors to provide the means for their privileged lives as opposed to doing for themselves. This perception of the world has amalgamated into an idealistic vision of American policy, where the government can simply transition into a new role as a *provider,* as opposed to an incentive promoter. Such ideas have established themselves as the new political platform called *"Democratic Socialism"* - where popular presidential candidate Bernie Sanders drew such support.

What is True Capitalism?

Many of the arguments of these Democratic Socialists are grounded in the defamation of some misconstrued idea of *capitalism*. To set things straight *capitalism* simply means market freedom, which means giving the power of success into the hands of "we the people." It is that equal opportunity I mentioned. It is choice. It is NATURE, in that we compete because the best man must win. It is a framework that is conducive with how the world WORKS. Our minds are awakened by competition, ambition, and success. The fact that you have a political argument implies that you think you are correct, which implies an ego and a competitive drive. Such an idea is inescapable!

On top of this, many who argue under these platforms don't consider themselves true socialists; rather, they have fallen under groupthink, where it seems "intelligent" to argue *against* a multisyllabic word (capitalism). They are quick to attach a negative connotation to anything associated with conservatism. This is because the media has done such a proficient job at generating emotionally charged narratives with a specific political rhetoric as opposed to remaining objective (as the media should do) - the media preys on the young and the ignorant.

Many young people are now quick to blame the idea of capitalism for the problems of the world like pollution or "global warming" or greed. They are blaming some abstraction of an idea that, in reality, only exists in their mind, and does not correlate with the nature of our economic system in America. This leads many youths into making a habit out of blaming institutional structures for the world's problems, instead of understanding that we, as people, cause the issues. This also means that it is in our hands to solve the issues we create, and America provides the

America provides you the opportunity to do just this: when there is an issue, you can fix it.

opportunity to do just this. Trying to fix the issues by dreaming up some socialist system that takes away your individual opportunities to fix things just doesn't even make any sense; nor does blaming some abstract, low-level understanding of "American Capitalism."

> *Socialism is when government's taking care of you:*
> *you send all your money to the government; the*
> *government decides how to spend it instead of*
> *letting the people spend it*
> *and make all those decisions.*
> *~ Bob Latta*

Instead of trying to change a system that is proven to work, the younger people of the U.S. can get a head start by embracing our framework. If you see a true problem in the world, then you can start a business to fix it. If you think medical costs are too expensive, then you can study medicine, and learn how to make our medical systems cheaper and more cost efficient.

These are problems waiting for us, the younger generation, to fix, but instead, we're screwing around with trivial political arguments, bashing a president who is setting up an economic climate that will only mean prosperity for you and me. Think of the greatest innovations of today - they all came about because of the freedom of capitalism. Whatever device or medium you are using as you read this book was afforded to you by just such a system.

The Natural Mindset of Capitalism

Unfortunately in this world, life is simply not a privileged situation. We don't get a pass to do whatever we want. Even if you are born into the idealistic financially well-to-do family, your mind will find ways to become discontent if no purpose for your existence is ever found. It is ingrained in our DNA to be productive as that is what our ancestors have done for thousands of years. Remember, life with the ease and comfort that you and I know is a relatively new phenomenon in the world. Not long ago, humans were going out and working dusk until dawn up until the beginning of the 20th century to essentially survive - easily evidencing why life is ingrained with the inherent property to sustain itself. Humans are based on productivity in one way or another.

What does this mean for *you*? This should help you understand the nature by which your mind operates. In all humans there is a drive to find some form of importance or success - be it in a social manner, a business manner, or in many other ways. This implies competition as a byproduct. We should not apply negative connotations to competition, for competition should ultimately lead to the greatest outcome. You can succeed in competitive environments if you possess a mindset of perpetual growth, even through failure.

Many young people are enticed by great orators like Bernie Sanders, who harp on the "rich" and the successful. Rather than going out and seeking methods of change, we now have groups of young people who would like to throw even more burdens on the successful people who already do their part in society. These motivations can be changed if we realize that those "successful" people *worked* for what they achieved, and that YOU and I can do it too!

Arguments can be made for how to change our healthcare and our education systems, and such debates should continue, for these are critical problems in America today. But we must NOT allow the "solutions" to these arguments to impede upon the overall capitalist structure of America, for it is <u>this </u>type of freedom that allows the citizens of this country to create, change, and succeed based on their skills, work ethic and ambitions. If the capitalist incentives are changed, you will see the population shift to looking towards the government to provide the means to our wellbeing, which ironically, is simply a roundabout way to squander our freedom.

> **I am a socialist and everyone knows it.**
>
> **~ Bernie Sanders**

The first step for us as Millennials, who are just now blossoming, is to accept these ideas, because we cannot outwit our natural instincts of competition, ambition and value. *The way to succeed in this world is to embrace the natural order of nature. Embracing your productive capabilities can lead you to a life of great achievement.* We must not fear failure, and we must not give ourselves up to the idea that those in the government have a much better grip on the world than we, the people, do.

> **Always bear in mind that your own resolution to succeed is more important than any other.**
> **~ Abraham Lincoln**

It is the Millennials that already do (or eventually will) understand these ideas - who will be the ones to shake off the generalizations about our generation. And for those who never accept these ideas, they will end up enjoying the fruits generated by the ones who *do* get it, but they will always maintain a life of mediocrity.

In America, the outcome of life is your choice;
do not listen to anything that tells you otherwise!

Reagan on Freedom

Freedom is never more than one generation away from extinction. We didn't pass it to our children in the bloodstream. It must be fought for, protected, and handed on for them to do the same, or one day we will spend our sunset years telling our children and our children's children what it was once like in the United States where men were free. You and I have the courage to say to our enemies, "There is a price we will not pay. There is a point beyond which they must not advance."

We'll preserve for our children this, the last best hope of man on earth, or we'll sentence them to take the last step into a thousand years of darkness.
~ Ronald Reagan

PART II:
GOVERNMENT BY THE PEOPLE!

The Door on the Right

In order to choose the Door on the Right, we must do an "about face" as a nation and go in a different direction on multiple issues. That requires our active participation in voting for those who will represent our traditional American values in Washington. It's time to boot out the Elites who claim to represent us, and bring our country back to "we the people"!

Steps to Make America Great Again

Exactly what steps need to be taken to make America great again? A great America is a strong America - an America that values basic freedoms for all citizens, respects the fundamental rights of all, and offers programs that will ensure victory, common sense, responsibility and the opportunity for success with dignity.

Let's overview two of the top areas that must see commonsense, creative changes. Then we will dive into some other crucial areas that need transformation.

Common Sense Immigration

We must, of course, protect our citizens from harm and danger. This means that we must secure our borders, rid ourselves of any illegal immigrants who are criminals and law-breakers, and establish a tight reign on legal immigration as well - at least in the short term.

It is not enough to simply welcome immigrants into our land. Time and solid data has shown us that we can, indeed, welcome those who are thoroughly vetted, and those with skills our country can use, and above all else, those who want to become true Americans. These immigrants _want_ to obey our laws, embrace our beliefs, and shun any foreign ideology they may have known that is anti-freedom. Those who cannot do these things have no place here. Legal immigrants need to be givers as well as takers.

Job Creation

Perhaps our most important task as a country is massive and healthy job creation. When achieved, this will go a long way to decrease many other national giveaway programs which are now bloated and debt-ridden - promoted to help those who cannot find decent jobs *because* of the very socialistic policies that have been promoted and implemented!

The truth is, we will NEVER have decent job creation under the policies of socialism. Why not? Because to do so would violate the socialists' personal ideology of government (and freedom) and would leave behind Constitutional government - the *"government of the people, by the people and for the people"* – a phrase referenced by Abraham Lincoln in his famous Gettysburg Address.

Below I have outlined 6 steps for job creation that would continue to propel growth in this area. Let's take a look.

6 Steps for Robust Job Creation

There are 6 steps that the U.S. Government should take to re-establish good and plentiful jobs in America. The first four are absolutely essential - the last two would be extremely useful also.

1. Remove the unjust regulations on business, especially small business, so that more people and groups can start and expand businesses, with reasonable risks.

2. Repeal Obamacare entirely and set up a system using free competition in the marketplace - giving people choices about their own healthcare. This will lessen the cost of healthcare considerably, while also benefiting businesses (particularly small businesses, which are currently being crushed by Obamacare regulations).

3. Completely revise the tax code, lowering taxes on both big and small businesses, and bring back the money from overseas that is kept there by companies unwilling to pay the huge corporate tax rate of 35% (the highest in the world). Note: We are already seeing great results from the huge tax cut President Trump signed, which is making the U.S.A. more business-friendly once again.

4. Renegotiate all trade agreements with each nation so that, for once, the U.S.A. gets a fair shake

and its products can be exported to the fullest extent feasible. The present trade deficits with nearly all countries are killing our economy.

5. Strive for energy independence and then never look back (socialism has dragged its feet on this issue forever). Quit buying oil and oil products from nations who hate us (and in many cases, use our trade money to fund world terrorism).

6. In addition, make all efforts to develop natural and alternate forms of energy - and most importantly - never replace the energy forms we have unless and until these can do the complete job of replacing the proven energy sources upon which we already depend.

Tackling these two high-priority items first (common sense immigration and job creation) will do much to ensure the safety and stability of the American people.

In order to make America great again - proud, wealthy, safe and strong again, we need to see some big changes made in many different areas that have been in steady decline under the disastrous rule of socialistic leadership.

Let's take a closer look now at those **changes in government** that must be made and why. Many of these specific areas have already been impacted positively by President Trump's policies, and more changes are on the horizon. Note the stark contrast between the results of socialistic policy and the impact of conservative policies that, once put into practice, lead to more freedom, opportunity and prosperity. Yet we still have much work to do. Each area is important and plays a vital role in the recovery of health for our nation.

Make America Proud Again

Back to the Basics in Education

Proper and relevant education is another powerful area - one that has the ability to influence our people to become proud of their nation once again.

We must strive to educate our citizens, whoever they are and in whatever condition they are in, to become interested in their government and in its workings. They should be taught about the various parts of our government, such as the Congress, both houses, the Presidency and the Supreme Court, as well as the lower courts. It is an <u>absolute necessity</u> to teach our citizens – young to old - how this country was founded and why.

> **Eternal vigilance is the price of liberty.**
> **~ Wendell Phillips**

It is an old saying, but so strikingly true - *"Eternal vigilance is the price of liberty." (Wendell Phillips)* If we do not take care of our liberty, we will lose it - and some day it will be too late to get it back!

Grade schools, high schools, colleges and universities must teach the fundamentals of our country's structure, the three branches of government and their function. Then hopefully in the future we won't have young people who have no clue who fought in the Civil War, World War I or II, and so on (just watch a segment of

Watter's World on Fox News if you are unaware of the current state of our educational system in the U.S.).

Colleges and Universities should have <u>no</u> federal funds whatsoever unless they can <u>clearly</u> demonstrate that they are teaching these government fundamentals. What then what would happen to the liberal elite in many public universities? They would disappear, and the country would be better without them!

Note: There are many topics which go beyond the scope of this book, but if you are interested in the roots of some of our most famous universities such as Yale, Harvard, etc., do some research to find out how they were established when founded. They were God-respecting, conservative- principled institutions long before they became something vastly different from what the founders intended!

I also believe that we should greatly expand our good trade schools - those institutions that teach the skills of various trades and do so with excellence. Trades such as plumbing, electrical contracting, heating, cooling, architecture, carpentry, interior and exterior design, and so forth can be taught by skilled workers who would mentor the lesser skilled. This expansion would benefit the many Americans who do not intend to obtain a college degree or cannot afford one.

I would also like to see every course of training connected to every available type of job, including an offer of a range of potential income for each job or position.

It need not be 100% accurate, but at least a student could have a good idea of what they might expect to make from a particular job or line of work.

It is a high crime, in my thinking, for a young man or woman to go into serious debt for a four to six year university program - costing in some cases $100,000 to $200,000 or more, only to discover that there are no jobs in their field to be had - largely because of the deplorable state of our recent job market and the job-killing policies of the socialists. Some of these talented young people have ended up working at minimum-wage or low–paying jobs totally unrelated to their years of study and sacrifice, and while still shouldering a nearly inconceivable amount of debt.

Make America Wealthy Again

Prioritize Job Creation

Lack of jobs is a direct result of downgrading the middle class. We have gone through a number of years of a horrible job market. If you are a person who can't find a job, whether within your training and skills or not, you are in big trouble and need. What happens to your family? You will probably end up being dependent upon government welfare without a job to support you. But you will get just enough to keep you under government help, with no improvement over that. What happens to your responsibility as the breadwinner - where is your dignity? What happens to your satisfaction, your self-worth, your hopes and dreams? Do these things not affect your freedom?

We have seen employment numbers rise dramatically under President Trump's leadership, while at the same time, we've seen a drastic decrease in the number of Americans on food stamps. With the robust job creation policies Trump supports, in addition to many companies returning from overseas and manufacturing in the U.S.A making a comeback, we know we are on the right track and we must keep this leadership in place to make continued progress! Of particular note is President Trump's statement that African-American unemployment numbers, in addition to Asian and Hispanic unemployment reached (as of the fall of 2018) the lowest levels in recorded history. And this is just the tip of the iceberg.

A Blueprint for Reviving Our Inner Cities

OPERATION INNER CITY RESCUE

This one potent idea could possibly make president Trump's presidential tenure the most dramatic, unusual and absolutely productive of all time. I could have called this section "solving cities' problems", but I think it is much broader in scope than that title indicates.

I know that President Trump has long decried the devastating crumbling of inner cities like Chicago, San Francisco, New York City, and others. What can be done to fix these decades-old problems?

Cities such as these that are in such bad shape are largely due to Socialist Democrat rule over such cities for up to 50 years or more. And this Democrat rule is, and has been, as wrong, careless and uncaring toward humankind as a ruling force can possibly be. The results are evident, factual and measurable.

The whole matter can be boiled down to the failed experiment of implementing socialism in these cities - pushing policies of vote harvesting, yet not truly caring for individuals who are stuck in the system. The Left will, of course, blame someone else or some other event, or the failure of others in power before themselves, or possibly admit that they tried and failed because the Republicans wouldn't vote for the money to do thus and such. But the problems of many of the big inner cities are largely problems of a Democrat-Socialistic ruler-ship, and as such, they will not simply disappear given more time.

I am proposing a bold plan to rescue the men and women caught up in such a system. What I am proposing is just an idea and an outline of what could be done. There is no question but that something **must** be done to rescue the people in these forgotten cities. Many (but by no means all) of these people are minorities.

Here is a brief outline of a potential plan. Please hear me out before passing judgment on the practicality or feasibility of such an undertaking.

A partnership could be formed between each participating state and the Federal Government. Only those states that could demonstrate serious problems with their inner cities would be considered.

All of the essential funds would come from the Federal Government, and there would be no conflicts of interest and no intrusion upon states' rights. Each state involved would decide to partner or not - their choice. In the beginning, there would be no time limits to either begin or to end. The entire system would be voluntary.

With many, many Republican governors now in state offices, it would be a great time for a test run of this plan.

For those concerned about the cost of such a program, please consider the millions that have been removed from the welfare roles since the new tax cut was passed, the billions we are now saving by opting out of unfair trade deals, and the drastic improvement in the economy under our current President. I believe the benefits far outweigh the costs.

The jobless, the forgotten, the unfortunate and disadvantaged people could sign up for this program. At appropriate times, jobs could be found for such people, perhaps related to ongoing infrastructure work or other local job opportunities. No one would be in any way forced to engage in any program, whether federal or state.

The federal leaders may suggest guidelines and procedures, but with no hard and fast regulations - because all will be concerned with the out-of-job and out-of-opportunity people who need help and hope for the future.

I would also strongly advise that the Federal Government provide instructional videos about our laws and the uniqueness of our country. Seminars could be given (even in a very basic format), and movies developed that would target professional behavior and job skills as well as ways to complete work and honor employers. I believe we would eventually see a notable difference in work attitude with this type of education.

Individual states could sharpen and improve on the ideas set forth here. Cooperation with the program would be the responsibility of the job seekers. They would be free at any time to leave the program, but with the clear understanding that they will be missing out on the benefits they could obtain by job training and opportunities for skill development with zero out-of-pocket expense.

Some temporary housing, clothing, and perhaps one hot meal per day, either furnished or paid for by the government may be needed. Before some scream about the expense of all this, please consider the expense of murders, riots, violence, looting, illegal drugs and citizen harm and danger. Also the fact that those we don't help now will become more expensive (and more hopeless) to help than if we had done nothing.

No state would be required to do anything or partner with anyone; no job seeker or help seeker would be required to do anything other than participate voluntarily. The best motivation is self-motivation, and such a program would attract those who want a better life, and are willing to take positive action to pursue it.

If an individual state wanted to use the federal system and even expand upon it, they could front some state money to cover the additional cost. I'm sure some of our incoming governors have ideas that would improve on those outlined here. If this type of program were promoted in an appealing way, emphasizing rehabilitation for out-of-hope people, there may be some outright sizable donations given, as well as an appeal for philanthropic money in the mix. We can't know what is possible until we try!

One of the greatest gains we could see in the lives of our people would be simply this - many of the previously out-of-work, downtrodden and unfortunate among us would be glad to say: "You know, we finally have a government who cares - no lies, no put-offs, no blame, no lip service. We could get to like a government like this."

"We are at last a people and not a statistic."

Most of us like illustrations and stories that help us to see truth in action - genuine truth wrapped in real life experience. My father, Thomas W. Figley, was a schoolteacher and a local school superintendent for many years. He spent a total of over 70 years in public school work. The following is a story from his life.

When my dad was Superintendent of schools in Dunkirk, Ohio, many years ago, a certain young man was released from prison (I believe for robbery or some similar type of offense). This young man wanted to return to high school in Dunkirk, but the school board there was highly skeptical of this move. Yet my dad convinced them to go along with the idea. He would have been a freshman or sophomore in school rank. My dad gave him a little credit for some instruction he had while in prison, and advised the boy of his golden opportunity to make good with a second chance. He took my dad's advice seriously. This boy graduated with his class, and went on to become a minister! Now one could say "Well, that's just one instance." But what an inspiring instance and what a huge gain for the young lad, his family and for society!

Inner City Help Needed

We have today, in far too many cities, seemingly hopeless situations running rampant. We know that sex crimes, gunrunning, illegal drug pushing and many other crimes are being committed, as we speak, in most inner cities. The concept of public safety has seemingly vanished from many of our inner cities!

I understand that it will probably be very difficult in some cases to make changes in behavior. This is where the government can come in with videos and movies that show the difference between a reasonably good life and a life of crime. The choice is up to the individual. But there are amateur and professional moviemakers who can depict realistic life in both ways (as a criminal, and conversely, as a productive citizen) who know how to illustrate this in dramatic fashion. I believe there are many gifted people who would be glad to use their skill set to help reverse a bad situation in a life, a city, and a community. What a calling this would be!

I also believe that to make an educational program of this type successful, law enforcement must be beefed up to protect participants and volunteers from those who would oppose this action. Violent protestors should not be permitted to destabilize efforts to improve the inner cities.

Liberal Mayors may not agree with any of this, and there may be some leftist pushback, but again, how will we know what can be done if we don't try?

Change Lives With Spiritual Help

What could be done for the down-and-outers in a spiritual sense? I suggest that a highly successful method of helping prison inmates could also be used in dealing with other groups such as the homeless, numerous jobless people and those who have been unproductive due to depression. *Prison Fellowship*, founded by Chuck Colson, is just one such organization. Why not find someone who has been engaged in this type of ministry and ask for valuable feedback and ideas? The underlying principle here is to connect the struggling and their troubles to Jesus Christ and his transforming power.

I'm confident that there are many Evangelical ministers who would be interested in this type of work.

They might be teachers, or make themselves available for counseling or participate directly in other ways. I am thinking out loud at this point - but several pastors who are Trump supporters might be interested in this type of work, including pastors such as Rev. Darrell Scott. Men like these could be great role models and mentors for this program.

In addition, let me specify that if such groups who can deal with spiritual matters can be found and put into place, this kind of program would have pretty free reign - but would not officially be a part of the jobs movement. And the government movies, videos and seminars, etc. could also cooperate to a degree with those people in charge of spiritual renewal. It would be a very loose arrangement, but not an official partnership. Why? Because with voluntary unity among sectors to solve problems and meet needs, much criticism and stone throwing may be avoided. Unity and cooperation among agencies, programs and ministries would be a powerful combination to create lasting improvement in the lives of so many people in our inner cities!

Restructure Tax Laws

The inherent vice of capitalism is the unequal sharing of blessings; the inherent virtue of socialism is the equal sharing of miseries.
~ Winston Churchill

We cannot overestimate the effects of a long overdue tax structure overhaul. But with socialism it will never be done - at least not without a big fight! We have allowed multiple businesses and many manufacturing and distributing companies to be shipped overseas because our business tax structure has been one of the worst (and highest) in the world.

A 35% tax on businesses is unacceptable and outrageous. So what happens? Business corporations close up shop in the U.S.A. and go to Mexico, China, India, and who knows where else, and the socialists will do nothing about it. Why? Simply because they don't want people to succeed - they want them under their thumbs, minding their rotten rules and getting their rank and rotten results. If and when you don't need big and intrusive, faceless government any longer, they (the socialists) are going out of business.

Donald Trump recently, with the passage of his huge tax cut bill, has axed through-the-roof corporate taxes and also lowered individual tax rates for millions of Americans.

The results? If even <u>half</u> of the companies who left would come back from overseas, this would create many thousands of jobs, and bring back money from foreign lands. These companies have no intention of returning at a 35% tax rate. It would seem like heaven to many in the poor and middle class if these jobs were to come back to our shores. And what about accomplishment and personal dignity? That comes back also!

Thank the Lord we have elected a president who has a proactive view on profit and prosperity for the millions of citizens of the United States!

Limit EPA Regulations

Even though this category may belong to the regulatory function of businesses, it deserves recognition. I am not suggesting that we need absolutely no environmental laws or guidelines - we do. But no real scientist would vouch for the number and type of EPA regulations we have seen during the previous eight years under Obama.

The volume and scope of the current EPA regulations are paralyzing enough to cause numbness in a totem pole! They are ridiculous and quite costly to our economy.

How does this affect the life of the average working man or woman? It kills jobs and opportunities for millions of job-needy people. Take for instance, approving an oil pipeline coming from Canada. This proposal could not get past the socialists in Congress - there have been just enough votes to delay or defeat these proposals, in addition to Obama's vetoes. His vetoes plus his executive action cast doubt upon the value of pens and phones he has used to suppress needed progress.

Embrace Energy Independence

This topic has been discussed for decades, with just a few steps being taken towards it. There are now vastly new and remarkable scientific methods of getting oil and natural gas into our hands - from our own land and our own resources. We have discovered new sources of energy hidden under our soil. True, it may take more expense to get it out, but oh, how important it could be to our future!

It will take time to fully become energy independent, so we will need patience. But if and when we become energy independent as a nation, we can become a much richer and more powerful nation than anyone may currently imagine. And eventually, the price of this new energy will be greatly affordable.

Can you imagine, dear readers, the vast number of jobs that could be created if true energy independence for the United States ever came to pass? It won't ever be allowed under socialism, because if it were, what would happen to the lives of all these people they (the socialists) have suppressed and downgraded? They would begin to prosper. The socialists just could not allow that. ***Way too many people would discover that they don't need a government that fills one pocket***

and empties another to do it. It would overturn their socialist agenda, and they know it.

Since Trump took office, great strides have been made in the area of energy independence, and we have also been pleasantly surprised at the announcement of the Space Force (another arm of the military). It's time we, as a nation, get back to the top of energy supply, research, and independence.

Pursue Alternate Forms Of Energy

We already employ some forms of alternative energy, but to depend on these forms of energy in huge quantities to completely replace coal, oil, electric and nuclear power, will probably require much more time and trial than we have used to date.

We should use these alternative forms of energy when feasible, but be very certain that this alternative energy is practical, affordable and completely safe and dependable before abandoning proven energy systems already in use.

It seems to me that the most recent socialistic leaders in government in the United States have thrown these alternative energy forms at us as if they are completely ready to replace what we are currently using. In reality, the readiness, affordability, and practicality are not there yet. I secretly think that our socialistic government under Obama's leadership was looking for ways to control or experiment on us, the Common People, by the use of untested alternative energy sources. What are your thoughts?

Ditch Obamacare

Without question, "Obamacare" is one of the biggest disasters of the century. Why? Because it doesn't work - it has <u>never</u> worked - it <u>can never</u> work!!

Why is this? The answer is simply because, from the very beginning, the idea of government-run healthcare was built upon a false idea - *division of wealth*. Many younger folks would sign up for the fiasco and would make up the money deficit of the older people, or so we were told. What a great idea - some would get something for very little or for nothing, and other people would pay for it. Division of wealth as long as you live, and ***you pay for it.***

We pay for those who have no insurance, whether they are motivated to work or not.

And, of course, there is just one plan for all, no difference. Plus a steep penalty was imposed if you did not sign up – regardless of whether or not you could afford it (thank the Lord that President Trump reversed that penalty since he took office).

"And besides all this"... (The Bible says in a particular New Testament story from Luke 16), *"Between us and you a great chasm has been set in place, so that those*

who want to go from here to you cannot, nor can anyone cross over from there to us.'" (Luke 16:26, NIV)

The "great chasm" comparison in this healthcare scenario is the reality that the Obamacare program can't work - because it was built on lies to begin with. Obama told us that the average family would see lower premiums that would save them up to $2,500 per year on his health plan. The reality is that, for many, the cost is up to $3,500 to $4,000 *more* per year than the individual was paying before. And Obama also said that you could keep your own doctor - oops!! Wrong again!! In many cases you cannot!

And – are you ready for this? (Imagine the benefits of his "one-size-fits-all" program) - would you believe that Obamacare policies for 90 year-old men cover **pregnancy?** Now if it is possible to be more stupid than that – please show me how!!

In addition to the above disasters, many insurance companies are getting out of the Obama plan because they are losing money. Now folks, is that real progress?

Let me ask you sincerely, dear friend, how has Obamacare served you?

It's way past time we injected common sense into this discussion and promote healthy competition between insurance companies again. Government run healthcare has been a colossal failure!

Make America Strong Again

Restore Government Stability

We all want stability. Yet socialism will never give us true stability. Why? Their basic ideology is contrary to it. An unstable government cannot ensure safety, strength or job satisfaction. <u>Socialistic governments have to spend more than they take in for revenue because of the price of their giveaways</u>, in addition to the fact that the middle class is job-poor. The victims of socialism will eventually be forced to accept less and less government help. A vibrant middle class (good job wise) would provide a huge part of the government's needed revenue for necessary programs and not just provide assistance for the disabled. But the middle class, beaten down by socialistic principals, can never supply this.

We are finally beginning to understand what it feels like to become strong as a nation, and respected once again by other nations around the globe. We no longer have a leader who takes "apology tours" around the world. Instead, we have a brilliant negotiator- a tough-but-fair President who encourages the world to live in peace, yet insists that we as a country are also treated fairly. President Trump often asks at his rallies: "Are you tired of winning yet?" I can definitely answer that

I will <u>never</u> tire of winning. I like winning much better than losing!

Correct the Balance Of Trade Deficits

This has been a problem that has gotten worse since NAFTA has taken effect during Bill Clinton's Administration. Granted, this didn't begin with Obama, but Obama did nothing about it. It has now reached the point where we clearly see that we should have helped other countries build their societies in another way.

Our current trade system "imbalance" has helped all those with whom we trade, but has been a huge negative for the United States.

Donald Trump says that the balance of trade system under NAFTA has left the U.S.A. with a total balance of 800 **billion** dollars in negative trade. I know of a lot of systems that are beneficial to both parties - but NAFTA, as it is now, is, frankly, a disaster to the United States.

Now for us ordinary folks, how does this affect you? Simply put, if some improvement against negative trade could be negotiated with each of our trading partners, it could mean *millions* of jobs to produce products to be exported, the potential of thousands of factories built (or brought back to life) to make those products, and a stabilizing effect on the job market which would be astounding.

However, massive trade imbalance fits the blueprint of the socialist agenda: keep the middle class poor, distraught and dependent so they will still remain under government's thumbs.

Along with the balance of trade deficit issue is the fact that the globalist agenda (a hallmark of the socialists) skyrocketed during the 8 years of Obama's tenure. When we agreed to the North American Free Trade Agreement, we were, in essence, flying high the globalist flag as opposed to the flag of our own nation. NAFTA was supposed to be a small way to aid disadvantaged countries with trade. But as a nation we have suffered great loss because of NAFTA.

Highlighting just one of the many flaws of the socialistic agenda, NAFTA has never done anything positive for us, per se. We, as a country, now know that globalism works **against** any country that has anything, as it gives away its money and advantages to others.

Need more proof? Go do a little search engine research on what is happening in Venezuela - the heartbreak and suffering of those people under a socialistic system is a nightmare in reality.

Even the less fortunate folks were being forced to contribute something to the NAFTA system. In essence, all American taxpayers were paying for this failed agreement that offered no benefit to our people. The truth is that most countries are taking, but not giving. There were many who worried that this would happen when

NAFTA was adopted, and now their concerns have become stark reality.

So, here we are... Our generosity has gained us little but loss of money, loss of U.S. jobs and a weakening of U.S. influence in the world. We cannot continue to give up our good markets to those who ravage our good intentions and don't give anything in return.

It is admirable to be compassionate - but when your country is being destroyed by your "compassion" in trade, it is time to get rid of NAFTA for good, or redefine the terms to make it fair for all countries involved. Thank you, President Trump for recognizing this travesty and doing something about it!

Compassion without common sense does not work. There must be some order and benefit to it. We can be compassionate as individuals and give to those in need, but when international agreements are entered into which may help others, but neglect our own people, is that really compassion?

Trump's tough talks on trade are necessary in order to get back to fair agreements for all. We just cannot expect other countries to be happy about that initially, because they are used to taking advantage of the United States and may have no desire for fair and balanced trade after years of getting their own way and dominating by default!

Rebuild Our Depleted Military

For a people who are free,
and who mean to remain so,
a well-organized and armed militia
is their best security.
~ Thomas Jefferson

Rebuilding our military is way too long overdue. We cannot expect victory if a vast part of our airpower and other military equipment is too old to do the job. Let's get to work with our officers and Congressional representatives who value a dollar and see how we can modernize. Obama has failed us here - and not only because of our weakened military - but because his anti-American ideology ruled his tenure. I realize this is a strong statement, but prove me wrong if you can.

And while we're at it, let's encourage some younger people to get into the military and learn some dignity, and find an honorable way to support themselves.

Enemies (whether entire countries or individuals) inherently understand strength - strength that can and will overpower them if necessary. It is called Peace through Strength - Reagan promoted it, and so must we. The improvement in morale and budget for the military since Trump took office is encouraging indeed!

Mandate Teaching On the U.S.A.'s Founding, Along With How Things Work And Why

Grade schools, middle schools, high schools, and all forms of higher education should be <u>required</u> to teach what makes America different and great. The Constitution must be explained and taught at <u>all</u> levels of learning – and schools who resist should get <u>no</u> federal funds whatsoever. Then government can turn the other problems of education back to the states and to the people, where they belong.

> **Give me four years to teach the children and the seed I have sown will never be uprooted.**
> **~ Vladimir Lenin**

Embrace Common Sense Education

I have already stated that we must teach the principles of our government: how it came to be formed, its structure, and its responsibilities to the citizenry. This should be required teaching at all levels of learning, beginning with kindergarten. This means that we get rid of Common Core, which is simply another liberal idea that the government has attempted to force down our collective throats.

Along with this, what better time is there to teach civility - compassion within the laws of the land - and good old common sense? It is fine to teach facts and figures. But we need also to teach children and adults how to think, how to process information, and how to reach conclusions about life's challenges. This should also be part of the educational process.

Educate on the Duties of Government

There needs to be some clarification on this matter. I believe we have a right and a duty - at all levels of education - to teach the basic principles of the Constitution. The duties of the three branches of government must also be required learning. Our guaranteed basic freedoms must be taught and the ideas of the Founding Fathers should be studied as the very basis of the knowledge of our country and how it was founded.

What are the duties of government? To promote the General Welfare is a primary duty. Teach the primary duties and the authority behind them, and you won't harm the populace. Instead, you will plant good seeds that will produce a harvest of responsible citizens that will greatly impact future generations for the better.

This (in my humble opinion) in no way violates states' rights. Rather, it provides a strong foundation for states' rights. This used to be the standard for every public school in this country! The purpose of this teaching is to promote liberty, defense, and safety for our citizens.

Except for teaching how our government was founded and what it stands for, the Federal Government should not interfere in the rights of states in educational matters. The states are closer to the people than the Federal Government, and communities are closer to the people than are the states. Primarily state action concerning education will garner the best results.

Appoint Constitutionalist Supreme Court Nominees

There could be three or four Supreme Court vacancies (or even more) within the next four to eight years. Thank the Lord these will not be filled with Hillary's selection of judges. No matter in which court they reside, if judges legislate from the bench (make law rather than interpret law), they should not be nominated, or should be removed from service if they are already in place. Appointing Supreme Court justices who value our Constitution is vital. But history proves that the Constitution has not been honored in this regard by the socialists, nor will it ever be.

Stand By Our Alliance With Israel

After the backstabbing and betrayal of the Obama years of leadership, the United States of America has, once again, demonstrated our love and our loyalty to the great nation of Israel. It is so long overdue. We can only hope and pray that people will one day soon realize the tremendous value of the only true representative democracy in the Middle East.

Of course, we desire peace between Israel and her neighbors. But it is no easy task. And the media seldom reports how often Israelis are attacked within their own borders by violent and hate-mongering terrorist fighters. If you lived in a small state and multiple rockets rained down on you (sometimes on a daily basis), would you appreciate massive international pressure to "make peace" with those intent on killing you? Yet this is exactly what Israel has been dealing with for decades.

Now, let me be very clear on this point: the Palestinian state is associated with, and governed by, more than one terrorist organization, and they have stoutly refused through the years to disavow and completely divorce themselves from such groups of terrorists and their beliefs. And in addition to this - the Palestinian state absolutely refuses to acknowledge the right of the state of Israel to even exist - and they will tell you so.

Because of this, any treaty or agreement between the Palestinians and Israel cannot be trusted under current conditions. Why? Because it won't be honored by the Palestinian state! Their leaders are terrorists and liars and, in their present state, they will always be the enemies of freedom.

It is clear that the actions of the Palestinian state, observed through the years, shows who they are, what they are, and why. In truth, many Palestinian people themselves are suffering under the domination of their terrorist leaders. These leaders don't even blink at terrorizing other nations, or even their own people, when it suits their agenda.

Our support for Israel and our willingness to talk to all parties is a good start. We must never again turn our backs on the state of Israel. Under our current President, I don't believe we will.

Provide Quality Care for Veterans

It is an absolute shame that our war veterans have suffered terribly in the absence of proper care for their wellbeing. To face violence at war and then return home to face medical carelessness is completely unacceptable. The Veterans Administration is in a big mess, not only from lack of leadership but also for lack of organization, planning and will. There are probably many causes for this. Regardless of the possible causes, we must begin to revive it by designing a system that will work. There is no better way to do this than by hiring proven leaders to do the planning and implementation. Any organization that is treated as an afterthought will not give us a satisfactory product. Our war veterans deserve so much better.

I was quite intrigued by Mr. Trump's idea to give our veterans access to regular care and treatment in the following manner: if they could not be seen by a doctor or caregiver in the VA within a reasonable time, they could choose another doctor to treat them. This excellent idea works, and doesn't leave our honored veterans out in the cold when it comes to healthcare. Of course, the governmental liberals don't like this because it is outside the one-size-fits-all model of the Obamacare system.

It would be ideal to see increasing movement towards a real partnership between the Veterans Administration and private healthcare. I believe it would work, and as we are currently observing a rise in governmental leaders who are conservative and highly successful, I do believe the job will be done correctly. Our highest priority should be to honor our veterans with the utmost quality of care.

I have never had government services from the VA, but as a veteran of World War II, I have a great degree of interest, concern, and insight into this issue. I will be following this matter very closely.

Respect States' Rights

We are stronger as a nation when we follow the blue-print our Founding Fathers laid out for us. A federal "power-grab" was never envisioned by our earliest Patriots – in fact, they warned us against this very possibility!

The provision of the U.S. Constitution, found in the Tenth Amendment simply says this: *"The powers not delegated to the United States by the Constitution,* **nor** *prohibited by it to the States,* **are reserved to the States respectively, or to the people"**.

This is an important provision in our laws, as there are many such powers that would be better handled by the states themselves. For example, activities not involving the U.S Government or our relations with any foreign country (such as issues close to home and family in local communities) are best handled by the states. I see no sense in the overreach of the Federal Government (which I have observed since World War II was ended). Of course, during any period of active war, the Federal Government must lead.

Individual states, in my opinion, have been pushed to the side of the road (in far too many instances) in preference to the one-size-fits-all entrenched system of the U.S. Government. The result of it all is obvious to any student of politics. Bad policies, steeped in government regulation, add unnecessary complexity and challenge to getting things done. Issues involving laws that have no national bearing have no business becoming national issues. I choose here not to be specific because if the guidelines were even partially observed, the Federal Government would be automatically sending these issues to the states.

I have observed that the more socialistic a president is, and the more he forces his liberal agenda, the more states' rights are infringed upon. During the eight years of the Obama debacle, many states' rights were outright stolen, and needlessly so. More states' rights, where appropriate, would result in much more local satisfaction.

Reduce the Size Of Government

A government big enough to give you everything you want is a government big enough to take from you everything you have.
~ Gerald Ford

The Federal Government, with its tremendous size and scope and its bloated debt-ridden belly has become a monstrous disaster. It is a fact that most of Obama's "job growth" was adding government jobs by the thousands. Now the question becomes - what was the result of all of that? Did our feeble economy boom during his tenure? Hardly! And yet there was little mention of this by the mainstream media or the Democrat leadership. What a coincidence (tongue in cheek)! Of course, socialism is like that! It seems to me that a massive increase in government jobs is not exactly a formula for job production. Job creation in the private sector is what we should be looking for - jobs that can continue on and on for years, and not be subject to political fallout.

Simply giving away jobs in order to get elected (at the taxpayer's expense) is not what we need. We want a slimmer, trimmer government, with bright and energetic people, knowledgeable people, people of dedication, folks determined to make our Federal Government into a responsible entity that upholds the Constitution and our by-laws. Honoring our roots and bringing government back to what our Founding Fathers intended would return us once more to one of the greatest nations on earth.

> **A government big enough to give you everything you want is a government big enough to take from you everything you have.**
>
> **~ Gerald Ford**

Government that is too big produces a number of bad results: confusion over whose authority is whose, great opportunities to create mischief and unnecessary regulations, duplication of effort, and certainly the temptation to entrench bloated power-hungry bureaucrats – this was never envisioned by our Founding Fathers. There are also many other undesirable effects of huge government, one of

> **Government is like a baby. An alimentary canal with a big appetite at one end and no sense of responsibility at the other.**
> **~ Ronald Reagan**

which is promoting even bigger government in order to satisfy the lust for power and scope in a system already too bloated and corrupt.

Require Term Limits For U.S. Senators And Representatives

I firmly believe the time has come for this vital step in democracy to be enacted. At least the usual term limits for President have been observed at two, except for Franklin D. Roosevelt. So why not term limits for the rest of the elected officials?

It would seem appropriate at this time for us as a nation to limit terms. One suggestion is for two terms of six years each for Senators and three terms of two years each for House Representatives – this seems to be about right in my view. Even something similar to the above guidelines would be a great improvement over how we currently operate.

The reason for term limits should be quite obvious. There is and has been entirely too much entrenchment, as many stay in leadership positions for thirty years or more. This was certainly not the objective of the Founding Fathers. Senators and House Representatives are making a career out of politics, and it shows up in what is being done and what isn't being done in Congress. More and more corruption is being exposed - and we are just beginning to see how those in the "Deep State" bow to lobbyist money and agree to hide improprieties of all kinds - including those actions that put our country and people at an alarming security risk! These positions were never intended to be a permanent career.

Why are term limits needed, some may ask? Term limits would bring in new ideas, many of which may shed new light on ways to govern wisely and preserve our Constitutional freedoms and values. There would be little likelihood of any Senator or House Representative making a career out of being reelected all the time, and more motivation to get things accomplished that would lead to a smooth-running government, and a positive legacy for those who get elected. They may well be much more motivated to fulfill their campaign promises, and leave the country in better condition than it was when they were voted into office. What a concept!

I also believe that members of Congress must spend at least one term out of office before running again.

Term limits would allow for less and less entrenchment in either position. Also, part of the new law could specify that a Senator or House Representative, having served his or her legal term limits, could not run for the opposite office either. One term out of office would be required. Those currently out of office, under this system, would be welcomed back after the time period is up, but many might find it difficult to start again, or unwilling to spend the time and money. This could perhaps give our country a little more balance than it has now.

Respect Religious Liberty

I am aware that anyone who speaks boldly on this subject might be in for trouble - but let me be very, very clear. I refuse to be intimidated. To me, it is worth the risk in order to foster a correct definition of what religious liberty is, and what it is not.

Too many people confuse liberty with license. But liberty can be quickly explained by filtering people's (so-called) liberty through the basic freedoms that our Bill of Rights sets forth. License is the legal right to do or say something. Liberty is the right of everyone to have a certain privilege. *If what you are doing or saying*

interferes with someone else's legal right, it should not be done - you have no license or right to do it.

Just because a person expects a certain outcome as a result of their words and actions doesn't necessarily mean it is legal or even appropriate. There is often a real difference between what a person wants for himself and what is legal for them to have and possess. The only accurate filter is to refer to the basic rights guaranteed to us by our Bill of Rights, which is equivalent to our Constitution.

We must assume that the basic rights given to us - woven deeply into the very fabric of the foundation of our country, a democracy within a Republic of the United States of America, applies to <u>all</u> of our people.

It is true that religious liberty gives each person the right to believe in any deity they choose, and observe any type of religious practice they want to observe.

However, with this so-called "right", the practice of any and all types of religion must never, in any way, shape or form, violate the Constitution of the United States, or any provision thereof, or any state or federal law on the books. This would include a ban on encouraging others to violate or ignore our Constitution, which protects the basic rights of all people. There must be no law or custom practiced by anyone that violates our Constitution or any settled law based upon it. Thus there can be no Sharia law or any other practice (whether foreign or domestic) encouraged or permitted that would violate our Constitution - in precept or in actual practice.

I personally believe the following parameters should also be considered.

It is all right to practice customs in private, but see to it that such practices never promote having or gaining precedence over any U.S.A. law (state or federal) that is based on our Constitution.

I would like to assume that an immigrant coming to the United States would never think of advocating any law or regulation that would override the Constitution of the U.S.A. If they did so for long, they should not be tolerated here. Trampling the rights of others is not a basic freedom!

If someone wants to become a U.S. citizen, then they must agree to follow the laws of the U.S.

Yet, I see evidence that ideas are emerging among some - ideas that are directly opposed to our Constitution - that are also contrary to the basic rights of an individual.

Folks, if a person desires to come into the U.S.A. legally, we would hope that they are coming here to become good American citizens. If they are not, they have no right to come. Simply stated, if someone wants to become a U.S. citizen, then they must agree to follow the laws of the U.S.

We are seeing a restoration of religious liberty take place since President Trump has taken office. Those who practice their faith (when it is not contrary to the Constitution) should never be treated as second-class citizens or targeted for government harassment (as they were by the IRS in the Obama years). This country was founded on Judeo-Christian values and ethics and we must return to our roots. We fled England in order to pursue religious liberty. We dare not turn our backs on the very reason our country was founded in the first place!

Regarding Legislation From the Bench (Judges)

What exactly does this mean? If this isn't clear, the results can be devastating. There are, unfortunately, many judges on the Federal Bench in particular, that tend to **make** law rather than **interpret** law. It would be good for the country if such judges were called out, and possibly recalled from their position. I am not sure that attempts to do so would be successful, but there should be a method implemented to address this serious concern. Of course, because of the difficulty of such action, probably not all guilty judges could be removed. But if they knew there would be some accountability for how they perform in their office, perhaps they would think twice before acting against the Constitution and creating mayhem by enacting their own version of the Law.

Make America Safe Again

The function of socialism is to raise
suffering to a higher level.
~ Norman Mailer

Repair Crumbling Infrastructure

This massive problem is one that President Obama paid little attention to during his terms in office. Crumbling infrastructure goes hand-in-hand with crumbling foreign relations, a crumbling job market, a horrendous national debt, the crumbling confidence of voters looking for some kind of government transparency, and also (I might add), a crumbling national will as well as a crumbling Field of Dreams for far too many Americans.

The time will always come when the crumbling infrastructure of a county, a city, or a country, will come home to roost, and something drastic will have to be done. I am referring to roads, sidewalks, public buildings, parks, public recreational areas, rivers and everything else that our citizens touch daily. What about bridges, sewer lines, and railroad lines, along with hundreds of other foundational infrastructure essentials? We travel over roads and bridges daily, and many are simply no longer safe.

This is yet another area that socialism tends to ignore - socialists are happy to spend a fortune on whatever they perceive will bring votes to those in power, but very little on safety and comfort of the citizenry. Socialism is indeed a powerfully destructive form of government - not only because of what they **will** do to erode our freedoms - but also for what they **won't** do to preserve our safety and security.

What do you suppose might happen if we got into a war with a foreign enemy or were swept up in some other national emergency and our roads became clear hazards for the moving of goods?

Of course, the rebuilding of infrastructure includes repair, rebuilding and replacement, and whatever is necessary for practical longevity of vital roads, buildings and public areas. And yes, it will take a lot of money. But on the other hand, it can't be delayed a lot longer. This project should and must create a lot of jobs. Therefore, more working taxpayers and more hazards corrected will cover part of the expense.

Road and building contractors can coordinate on the details of how best this gigantic task can be accomplished. We want the best repairs possible with the least expense involved. Many jobs will be created, both permanent and temporary. If at all possible, jobs may be offered to as many jobless as is feasible with minorities getting their fair share. Trained leaders of teams could be appointed to train the lesser skilled, so that people can be paid while they learn a marketable skill.

Donald Trump has made the rebuilding of this country's infrastructure a major campaign issue, along with a whole host of other vital issues. Our dilapidated infrastructure is indeed the "elephant in the room," and I applaud our leadership for their willingness to tackle this monstrous problem. Now we must hold the members of Congress responsible to pass (and not stall) measures that will highlight solutions and implementation of the restoration of our infrastructure.

I sincerely believe that under President Trump's leadership, this great task will be accomplished and viewed as a resounding success. And if other jobs are being created at the same time, a massive number of people will gain work, money and a sense of dignity.

Revisit Immigration Reform

So many people are so incensed over the entire subject of immigration reform. I do not dispute the fact that there are different viewpoints on this subject, some widely different from others. But we must start somewhere. Let's take into account safety, fairness and feasibility and make necessary changes.

First of all, the socialists, many of whom have been running our government, and any who may come after them, have to realize the very thing they don't want to admit, and that simply is this - our Constitution **demands** public safety. The Preamble of the Constitution lays out the duties of the U.S. government - to provide for the common defense, promote the general welfare, and secure the blessings of liberty to us and to our posterity. This is part of the fabric of our by-laws.

Now folks, it may be that our Founding Fathers did not envision a common defense of the type and magnitude of today, but I will ask you - what is the difference between the effect of a foreign army invasion of our country and the effect of illegal aliens, some of whom are criminally inspired, destroying the safety and well-being of our U.S. citizens?

There will be a radical difference in how many citizens we lose to violent death depending on the magnitude of the intrusion into our nation. Regardless of the murder rate factor, however, there is no doubt that un-vetted and illegal immigration will result in a loss of safety, wellbeing and security for our citizens – no matter where the safety threat originated.

Apparently, our socialistic leaders do not see this blatant truth, but I do. Regardless of who or what may create it, lack of security is a national problem. The socialists, with Hillary at the forefront, talk of "compassion" and "care" for illegal immigrants who break the law – but she and her cohorts never bother to mention the threat to public safety that is occurring even as she speaks. We cannot overlook our Constitution's insistence on the basic right of safety for our <u>own</u> citizens.

My, oh my!! Who is at fault there? Even if you don't like a law, you must respect it until it can be changed, and who would want to change public protection?

I will answer that question now. Those guilty liberals and socialists would include two categories of voters. The first category are those with a strong left-wing ideology, who do not care about the safety of our citizens - who would want open borders at all costs. And why would they want this? Simple - because they hate the rights the Constitution affords our citizens. The other category of voters are primarily younger people who were not taught how our country was founded nor what it truly means to be a free American.

Hard-line socialists would rather have open borders to show a misplaced compassion for unknown strangers - those whom they hope would then vote Democrat for their entire lives. Never mind the murder of citizens and even entire families of citizens by certain illegal aliens. And some of these violent crimes and murders are tied to illegal immigrants that have been deported 6 or more times and entered the U.S.A. yet again to perpetuate even more death and destruction!

But we might ask them, "Do you mean to say that a person's political ideology should prevail over law and order - over the protection of our citizens from harm and danger, even death?" Socialists might well answer yes.

But millions of law-abiding Americans said "NO!" with their ballots in the election of 2016. These immigration problems continue to be a hot topic in our current election cycle as well.

Sometimes you will encounter younger people who have no Constitutional knowledge, many of these being college-age, who can't seem to grasp the idea of safety first. There are some young people who can't even correctly tell you who fought in the Civil War or in the Revolutionary War. Was it Spain or France?

Dare we let people like this rule our country? I sincerely hope not!

Decades of leftist indoctrination force fed via our public schools have resulted in an alarming lack of knowledge about even the most basic of our country's founding freedom principles in many of our younger Americans. We must return to common sense in our educational system as well.

What is the solution to the situation of illegal aliens coming into our country, most of them streaming across the Mexican border with the U.S.? Simple. Build a wall! "Oh, but what a horrible act this would be!" some would say. Oh, really?

The Left's pretense of compassion puts our entire country at risk of eventual collapse; citizens are not safe, taxpayers (already near bankruptcy from unfair tax burdens) are crushed yet again, and violent crime rises, all from *pretending* that law and order is not important. It is not fair to put the burden of financial, economic and social responsibility for illegal border-crossers upon those law-abiding citizens who did not create the problem.

Why is immigration reform so vital? Some people may wonder why certain immigrants must not come here, particularly those who cannot easily be vetted or even vetted at all. Immigrant hopefuls must be clearly taught about our government and the requirements of U.S. citizenship. Some foreign or religious ideology is directly opposed to our Constitution. For instance, we **cannot** have Sharia law in this country. Sharia law is common in Muslim societies, but it is contradictory to the personal freedoms guaranteed by our Constitution. These two types of laws are absolutely and diametrically opposed to one another.

We already have college professors and many judges who make rules promoting socialism and Marxism, and are getting away with it without correction or punishment. The rules that women must live by under communism (and Sharia law) are horrible and oppressive. Yet we've had socialists like Hillary Clinton who (during her 2016 Presidential run) didn't blink at taking millions of dollars in "donations" from these very countries that treat women like slaves.

Most other countries (with very few exceptions) have laws restricting their citizens' freedoms unlike the

U.S.A. Why bring these people here to poison the world's best system of freedom? Have we lost our way? There are some types of government that can never be reformed.

Sharia law is just one of them.

If any immigrant does not become a true American in thought and action, we have a traitor on our hands - and in some cases, a criminal - and they are now embedded within our country. Of course, there is room for cultural differences in this great Melting Pot, which is called America. But our freedoms do not extend to those practicing laws opposed to ours – because these dangerous, oppressive laws threaten our citizens.

Perhaps it can be best understood in playground language. If you come to my backyard to play ball, you play by my rules or you go somewhere else. The same holds true with immigrants who wish to come to our land of freedom. If they don't like our laws and the freedoms we hold dear, then they can go somewhere else. They won't be happy here, and our goal is not to make them happy at the expense of our law-abiding citizens. It's only fair.

Let's Talk About a Wall

What kind of wall would you build? Well, you certainly wouldn't follow mainstream media's non-answers - otherwise the wall would never be built. Citizens would continue to be killed by illegal immigrant criminals, and the rest of the U.S. citizens would go broke! No - you would do well to consult with law enforcement (on the border) and with governors and former governors of those states that border Mexico, and see what they have to say.

Where a wall might not work well in a few border areas, you would have U.S. and Coast Guard boats, plus Air Patrol and select electronic devices needed to stop border crossings. This would do the job.

What might we do about illegal aliens who are already here? Here are my thoughts. I would trust the Conservatives who won in the 2016 election, as well as those Patriots who will be elected in the Midterms to do what is right and best, but we still need to let our voices be heard. <u>All</u> illegal aliens with <u>any</u> criminal record here or elsewhere would be deported. Once the wall is in place, then our Congress - with input from the voters - can decide what to do with the millions of illegal immigrants that Obama, or any other authority, allowed to come in.

Furthermore, I personally strongly favor no citizenship for any illegal aliens, even those who may have been here for some time. They should have no voting rights whatsoever, and should pay a fine for failing to follow the laws of our great country. Those who have green cards, or work permits can stay, but should not have citizen's rights to vote.

Of course, all of this would take some time to implement. But unless our country brings back as much security as is possible, we will still have problems with illegal aliens. You might envision this as a mammoth task. Yes it is, but it would be a much greater task <u>not</u> to take action and simply watch our country's freedoms disappear forever.

One other thing, good people of the United States, ignoring the rule of law and calling it "compassion" does not dare to come ahead of the safety and security of U.S. citizens. Those who favor illegal entry of foreigners over the safety and security of our citizens cannot be allowed to run our country.

Destroy Isis / Terrorism

This will not be an easy task. Obama's blunders and failures to act against terrorism within our country as well as outside our borders have made it much more difficult. But much can be done and some of it rather quickly! First of all, without announcing any plans or secrets, President Trump must assemble the most formidable group of generals and officers - most of which have been sickened by Obama's political posture and inaction. Note that I'm not saying that Obama did nothing - but if anything, it was a feeble attempt at containment of our enemy - not a daring push for absolute victory over radical Islamic terrorism. There, I have called our enemy what he is, by name… Obama never did, nor did his socialist empire.

Our great generals and military commanders have been chomping at the bit for years to get real victory over a sworn enemy. The U.S.A. can ally itself with those who are (literally) dying for relief from terrorists, and we can do it by providing air support, weaponry, intelligence, strategic maneuvering and with very few boots on the ground. We need not go it alone.

In less than 2 years in office, Trump's military has drastically reduced the influence of Isis around the world, and a solid plan to defeat terrorism continues to be implemented by our strong and honorable military.

In closing Part II of this book and before the trumpet call to action in the Conclusion, I'd like to quote from the leader of the free world himself – the powerful words of a personal rallying cry to all of us as freedom-loving American Patriots:

We will not bend; we will not break.
We will never give in; we will never give up.
We will never back down; we will never surrender,
and we will always fight on to victory!
We are one people, one family,
and one glorious nation under God.
~ President Donald J. Trump
10/04/18, Rochester, MN rally

Because we are Americans
And our hearts bleed red, white and blue!
And together we will…
Make America Wealthy Again!
Make America Strong Again!
Make America Safe Again!
And We Will Make America Great Again!
~ President Donald J. Trump

CONCLUSION

Here's Hope!
How to Eliminate Socialism
In Your Lifetime

The truth is incontrovertible.
Malice may attack it, ignorance may deride it,
but in the end, there it is.
~ Winston Churchill

During the entire course of this book, I have presented the faces and facets of socialism in as many ways as possible in order to highlight the wrongs of this destructive ideology. I have also outlined creative methods and ideas to reverse the damage that has resulted from years of governmental abuse towards its own citizenry. I wrote this book in order to warn current voters, as well as to educate both new and younger voters to understand the evils of socialism. I hope that I have succeeded.

We have examined the characteristics of socialism, the many wrongs perpetrated by it, the traits of a socialist, and the evils inherent in this form of governing. My goal has been to educate as well as to warn voters and inspire them to use their voice in their local communities as well as at the ballot box to bring this country back to its founding principles.

I have depended very little on outside sources of information, because my age, interest and experiences with life and government have led me to the facts and the conclusions I have outlined.

From the time the bulk of this book was written (2016), I am now pleased to report that progress is being made on numerous issues that are addressed herein. Who is the driving force behind the progress? Our duly elected President Trump. The economy is growing, a huge tax cut has passed, technical schools are making a comeback, our veterans are receiving more attention and care, unfair trade policies (decades in the making) are being reversed, corruption is being exposed all over the world, and the Constitution and her principles are once again front and center in the discussion about the future of our nation.

Do you like the progress that is being made? (If you listen to the Main Stream Media, you likely aren't even aware of any progress – so obsessed they are with hatred for our leader). Do you want our nation to return to higher taxes, fewer jobs, more corporate and political corruption, and more terrorism? Are you in favor of more illegal criminals permitted to roam free and terrorize the innocent, and socialist-leaning judges appointed who make law according to whim (or their pocketbooks) instead of in deference to the clear vision outlined by our founding documents?

My friend, you have a clear choice. If you have observed any improvement in our economy, worldwide respect for our country (aside from the Mockingbird Media), the path back to fair trade, and positive changes resulting for the forgotten men, women and children of the U.S.A., it is imperative that you let your voice be heard in the midterm elections. It is vital to vote in *every* election - for if you choose not to, you can be sure that your enemy will do whatever possible to undo every one of the positive changes we have seen.

We voted to give Trump a chance. He has fought valiantly against the press, radical groups and the Deep State every single day since he was sworn into office. The ability to get ANYTHING accomplished amid such chaos is truly remarkable. Yet more has been accomplished in the past year and a half than most presidents have accomplished in a full term or more.

Give him two terms to see what can be accomplished. Our entire Republic is at stake. Our faith, safety, and a conducive environment to pursue happiness is at stake, for there will be a swift and sure reversal of this progress if the Democrats (mostly socialists in either name and/or deed) regain the majority in Congress. Ignore the Main Stream Media (MSM). Do your own research. Don't go with the first page of a search engine's results or social media propaganda either, as they have, in fact, been censored to silence the voices of Conservative Republicans and Independents.

Think about the world you want to leave to your children and grandchildren, and then go out and vote. It is your right and your privilege. Support true Patriots and encourage others to exercise their Constitutional rights as well. We have one last chance to get this right and make America Great Again. May God bless America and may our progeny look back one day and say:

"Thank God for our parents and grandparents who refused to give up our freedoms, but instead chose to fight for them and for us. Thank God that we still have the right to life, liberty, and the pursuit of happiness. Thank God for His grace and help to root out corruption and turn our nation right side up again! Thank God for faith, family and hope for our future."

Now that you know the story behind socialism, my friends, I implore you to hold in high esteem a government which values freedom, and pledge to support it.

Even though we may not agree on every policy, our current choice is between Democrat-Socialism and the Republican Party. Vote for true Patriots to represent us in our leadership. Get to know the candidates and what they stand for and against. Register to vote. Vote in the primary elections as well as in the midterm and Presidential elections. The world will never have another government such as our Founding Fathers set up via the Constitution – a beautifully rich and unique type of governing intended to elevate freedom and ensure equal opportunity for all citizens.

If you pray, pray for those in authority that they will have the wisdom to lead us in peace and prosperity. Do what you can to support those candidates who will uphold our precious Constitution so that we may, once again, have liberty and justice for all.

In conclusion, I want to share the memory of my high school graduation valedictory address, where I ended my speech with a powerful poem from the well-worn pages of an old history book. Its timeless message is as true today as it has ever been.

The Torch of Freedom
It should be your pledge and mine to hold it
High like a beacon
Till our strong years be spent
And sinews weaken...
Till others in our stead
Take from our loosening hand...
The Torch - full streaming, which we pass...
At death's command.

William W. Figley
https://PricelessLifeInfo.com

AUTHOR BIOGRAPHY

William W. Figley, known as Bill by friends and acquaintances, was born on June 30, 1926, during the presidency of Calvin Coolidge. His father was a schoolteacher and later a superintendent in various public schools. His mother worked in a law office and attended college. Bill's high school years were spent in Southeastern Ohio where he participated in basketball, track, and high school plays.

Bill enlisted in the Navy a few months before high school graduation. World War II was ongoing and he served 30 days in the service of his country before the age of 18. He was discharged after the war with Japan had ended. Bill served as a signalman on a small amphibious ship, and traveled all over the Pacific Ocean area including the Hawaiian Islands, the Philippines, Mariana Islands (Saipan was a main city), Korea, Guam, and Okinawa, among other places. He was also inland into China.

After discharge from the Navy, Bill attended college at Ohio State University, and Ohio Northern University. Bill has owned various businesses over the course of his lifetime. For the past 25 years, He has been (and remains) a professional musician on the piano and keyboard. He is also an author and blogger who expounds on conservative politics and how these beliefs tie together with faith, family and the future of our nation.